Splinters

The Pain. The Passion. The Point.

By Barbara Howell

Splinters: The Pain. The Passion. The Point.

By Barbara Howell
ISBN 13: 978-0-9819879-0-3

Publisher's Note:
The events recounted in this book are shared from Barbara Howell's perspective. Some details may have been altered or omitted to preserve the artistic integrity of the story.

Published by Paige1Publishing
Tulsa, OK | Nashville, TN
www.paige1publishing.com

3rd Printing August 2011

Printed in the United States of America.

Credits:
Cover Design/Typeset: JP Jones of Paige1Media
Editing/Proofreading: Jeff Bardel

Additional copies of the book may be purchased by writing the address above or visiting the Web site at www.splintersbook.com

splinters: the pain. the passion. the point.

foreword

This is a story of courage, perseverance, and endurance. A story of one woman's incredible journey to success despite insurmountable odds and being cast into a profession suited only for men.

Who is this woman? My grandmother, Barbara Howell.

What made her remarkable?

Barbara was born in an era where medical care was a luxury. She suffered a childhood illness that robbed her of 70 percent of her hearing. This tragedy left her completely deaf in one ear, and with severe hearing loss in the other. This handicap was just the beginning of her struggles.

Through a series of personal and family tragedies, Barbara would often face the decision to quit or continue to fight. With each attack, she found herself still fighting. Spurred on by her remarkable grit, determination, and faith in God, Barbara refused to succumb to the circumstances.

These circumstances included both her children's divorces, her husband's bouts with devastating cancer and mental illness, her brother-in-law's multiple murder conviction, and her own inner struggles when left with the responsibility of a six-figure debt.

Barbara used these obstacles to climb up the ladder of success. Her one and only business strength was management knowledge. Having been a cosmetologist and owner of her own business, her knowledge was potent despite the fact that she had closed her business.

Thinking she was financially secure, she had enrolled in college with the intentions of pursuing an old dream. Then a family crisis struck and not only aborted her college career, but plunged her into a six figure debt forcing her to take up a business her husband had started: building wooden display cases for collectibles and keepsakes.

Overwhelmed. But honorable, Barbara quickly learned this new trade and carved out her own niche in the industry.

The niche she found?

Barbara got into hardwood and soon

A display of Barbara's cases at a local gun show in Tulsa, OK.

found contacts that could supply exotic woods such as Purple Heart and Brazilian Cherry. In time, her business took on a dimension of its own and Southern Ladies Showcases was born.

Today, she has over a dozen distributors of her product internationally. Her customers whom she's honored to consider friends, include celebrities, race car drivers, hobbyists and teenagers: each one unique, and each one important. Her display cases are housed in homes, businesses, and museums across the United States and around the world.

Within the pages of this book, you will struggle with Barbara through the early years, and later celebrate her successes.

This book is divided into 3 sections. In the first section, *Splinters*, my grandmother shares her personal life, the ups and downs that got her where she is today. In section two, *Armed and Dangerous*, her customers tell their stories and share the experiences they had with Southern Ladies Showcases. Finally in the last section, *Behind the Scenes*, Barbara not only shares the humurous stories but also catastrophes of her life on the road during her traveling years working trade shows, flea markets and festivals.

As part of her family, I sincerely hope you find this book to be an inspiration, an encouragement, and a stepping stone to your ultimate success. As my grandmother, Barbara, would say, "IT AIN'T OVER TILL IT'S OVER!"

—Jennifer Jones

"It ain't over till it's over!"

acknowledgement: Charles Howell

Days of preparation.

Charlie Howell, Barbara's husband, was born in 1940 and raised in a deep holler in the backwoods of Tennessee.

When he went, he attended a little country school located a few miles from the holler.

The winter months were about the only time he attended school regularly. His dad wasn't keen on book learning; he was more into farming. And trying to squeeze out a living for 11 kids on a farm, even back then, took a lot of farm hands. Therefore, he kept all his boys home from school during the planting and harvesting seasons.

Then one day, Charlie's destiny called. His older sister had passed into high school. Her school was miles away from the holler, and besides that, she had to ride a bus for a couple of hours. Daddy said, "one of the boys has to transfer with her."

Charlie got elected or volunteered, he doesn't remember which, to attend the big school of Bodenham with his sister.

He loved it and got right into his woodworking classes. He was soon operating power saws, sanders, and had been assigned a project. He was to make a case to hold keepsakes.

And despite doing factory work for 40 years, this preparation would birth "Charlie's Showcases", that in turn, would birth "Southern Ladies Showcases", soon to be followed by his son's business, named, "Howell's Woodwork."

Charlie was in the 9th grade when his knack for woodworking was discovered.

splinters: an introduction

The owner of Southern Ladies Showcases drove her 58-foot rig onto the fair ground. The festival's promoter turned to direct her to her show booth for the next 14 days. Instead, his hand froze in mid-air, and for seconds he stood motionless. His expression easy to read, his eyes darted from the big rig to the old lady who sat behind the wheel.

Barbara smothered a grin, halfway sharing his concern.

Finally, he pointed to his right without speaking. She nodded, and shot a quick glance toward her 15-year-old granddaughter, who was riding shotgun. Her confidence was immediately restored. Despite owning no driver's license, this girl had the expertise to back anything. Anything? Yes. This 58-foot rig or their 24-foot cargo trailer. JJ could put either one right where she wanted them. It was a gift. And neither disbelief, nor respect from the male chauvinist watching, moved her.

Barbara, JJ, Jennifer, and Jeannea, were southern ladies working a man's profession enduring their fair share of opposition. They had been thrown out of trade shows due to macho-men's jealously. They had quit at the end of a show day, dog-tired, to experience the shock of finding their rig gone. And worse, no one had bothered to inform them *why* or *where* their rig had been towed.

They had racked up speeding tickets by the dozen. They had walked unhurt from serious wrecks, and when their vehicles weren't driveable, they had their trailers towed to the next show.

Tough and focused, they were successful carpenters yet they gave all the credit to the Master Carpenter, who had walked on the sea of Galilee.

One of Barbara's "rigs". Truck, fifth wheel RV, and 10' cargo trailer. A whopping 58' total.

This picture represented Barbara's life in 1994.

shattered

In 1994 Barbara Howell wasn't a likely candidate for Business Woman of the Year. Her life was fragmented. Her emotions were threadbare. She often wished for a cliff to jump from as she tried to cope with a mentally ill husband, Charles, who had been diagnosed with a chemical imbalance and had undergone a total personality change. He was a wrecked man, suffering from a dangerous, delusional, victim mentality. Bipolar, triggered from severe trauma, was the explanation the medical profession had given Barbara. She had no rebuttal, for she was painfully aware that their last five years had been a roller coaster of one emotional trauma after another.

Despite all her husband's efforts and expenses, his older brother had gone to prison for arson and murder, racking up six life sentences. Trailing this tragedy, he, himself, had experienced radical prostate cancer surgery, robbing him of his sexuality and bladder control. This created a permanent chemical imbalance, igniting irrational behavior and violent mood swings. During these erratic episodes, Charles would pack his things and disappear for hours at a time with no intention of returning. As the violence continued to escalate and turn to abuse, Barbara was strongly advised to help him get settled into his own place. She rented him an apartment located minutes from their house.

Denying he needed medical help, her husband became more angry and spiteful when she finally sought treatment for him. Upon being dismissed from the hospital, he pitched his medicine, and went back to work, refusing to pay one bill or help her in any way financially.

This unpredictable behavior forced the transfer of household responsibilities to her. In their 35 years of marriage, he had always insisted on handling the money issues. She didn't have a clue how to balance a checkbook, and no time now to learn. She owed a house-payment of over $900 per month and a $2,000 pledge to their church-building fund. To make matters worse, she shared a $65,000 line of credit debt on an almost bankrupt business.

Discouragement often plagued her. Despite all her pleadings, her mule-headed husband refused to take his medication and stay under his doctor's care. It became a battle of wills. Arrogantly, he told her often, that it was none of her business if he wanted to be angry and smoke like a chimney. It was his life and he certainly had a lot to be angry about!

He often insisted she was just being misled by all this doctor stuff about a chemical imbalance. He didn't have a chemical imbalance. His doctors were just meddling in morality issues not honesty when they told her his smoking contributed to his health issues.

His attitude was that *she was stupid for believing these doctors. He didn't.* He constantly belittled her.

Therefore, stubbornly, in denial, he plotted on, thinking she would sooner or later let him move back home. He knew and she strongly suspected, sooner or later, she would have to for he held the trump card. And he flashed it often, by telling her she wasn't a competent enough driver to even get out of town much less make her own living—which was true. Her driving abilities left a lot to be desired.

E K A
C Z H S
K S R N H
D V K H C R
N S D V C H O
D C N K O H R S

Glasses like those Barbara kept on her car dash in the late sixties and used only when driving until she had the restriction removed from her driver's license. She paid the big price of ten cents for them.

Born in 1940, she hadn't even bothered to get a driver's license until she was almost 30. Even then, she was self-taught while living on the back side of nowhere. For three weeks, she mowed down bushes and sage grass on a regular basis, managing one day to take out the barn door. However, she did learn enough to pass the driver's test, but only then, by borrowing her sister's glasses. For years, her driver's license was restricted to eye glasses she didn't even own. When she initially failed the eye exam due to nervousness she secretly borrowed her sister's glasses. A short time later, with her new license in hand she walked out and gave the glasses back to their owner.

Her motive for getting her license that day wasn't to gain independence. It was so she could drive 18 miles to be with her mom without breaking the law. Her teenage brother was bedfast, dying of bone cancer.

Years later, she passed the eye exam and had the restriction removed from her license. Her *improved* eyesight may have satisfied the Tennessee State Law, yet it hadn't helped her driving ability.

It would have blown her mind if anyone had suggested that her future was mapped out with long distance travel, often working five different states per month. You see, Barbara has no sense of direction. None.

Powder Mill Hill Country Crafts. Note the beautiful rocking chair on top of the building.

The year 1996 was the pits for Barbara. She had taken over the showcase business when Charlie had abandoned it. She kept hitting walls, her spirit sometimes broken to the point of barely hanging on.

"Ouch!"

She screamed out in pain one hard and depressing day, and made a desperate grab for her shirt tail. She fumbled, and the shirt, along with stomach became tangled up in the belt sander. Angrily, she yanked her shirt free and gave the sander a fling followed by the battered showcase.

She glared down at the splintered mess on the floor. It seemed to mock her.

Her arms ached. Her patience was wearing thin. Her blouse was in threads and her stomach sanded smoother than any part of the crumbled showcase lying on the floor. This showcase business looked hopeless. She was either sanding her belly or dancing the two-step trying to hold the case with one hand, and the belt sander with the other. The job always ended in a slinging match.

She had been buying lumber from her Amish friends. They had shown her how to air-dry wood, and have some always available when she needed it.

This method had worked great until recently. But now, her business had grown to such a proportion that she needed wood much faster than the Amish way could supply. Some hardwoods took a year or more of air-drying to be workable. To supplement her lack of materials, she had been buying wood from a local lumber yard. It wasn't working. The problem? The poplar wood was lighter and softer than oak. It wouldn't hold the weight of the sander. It danced. It was partly her fault, for she didn't have the grip in her hands, or the know-how, to hold the light-weight wood while sanding.

Barbara was smart enough to know her body couldn't continue to take this abuse. She had to do something. Pain pushed her. Temper pushed her. Desperation pushed her. She headed for the shower, her mind in replay. Bits and pieces of her last conversation with an Amish friend raked her thoughts feverishly. She remembered that he had said something about getting hardwood in Huntland, Tennessee. Hardwood. That's where she was missing it! She had to get back into hardwood. Hardwood such as oak and hickory. She rashly decided she would go to Huntland.

Hurriedly, she jerked her clothes off and stepped under the spray of water. She screamed when the water struck her angry-red raw flesh. The pain refueled her senseless anger.

Five miles from her house, speeding on *her* way to Huntland, the imp harassing her mind asked, "Where is Huntland?"

The question began to hammer her mind.

"It's above Pulaski," she muttered aloud, unconvincingly. "I know it's next to Pulaski," she tried hard to convince herself, becoming more agitated by the moment. Taken hostage by stubbornness, she continued to drive her truck toward the small southern town located in middle Tennessee.

"Come on! Come on!" she hissed, pushing her memory frantically, no longer evading truth. Still, the contents of her conversation with the Amish man remained just out of her reach.

This picture shows the road Barbara was traveling the day she met Todd Yannayon, the owner of Powder Mill Hill Country Crafts.

One of Barbara's Amish friends shopping in their home town.

"Hrmph!" She flipped back into angry delusion, and mocked her fear. "Those Amish boys drive horses and buggies. It can't be too far from Pulaski!" She thumped the steering wheel in silent rage. "I'll find it!" Home delivery never once crossed her mind.

"What is the business name?" the imp persisted.

"W-what's the business name?" she stammered aloud, realizing, she didn't have the first clue! She stomped her brakes and jarred to a stop. Her lips quivered and her delusion was finally arrested.

She clutched the steering wheel oblivious to the fact she was in the middle of the road. "Barb, you are out of your mind," she raved.

A reactor by nature, she had pulled some daring stunts in these last two years of hell. But this one took first prize, she faced the brutal truth about herself. Here, she was racing toward some unknown town; searching for some nameless business! How far out could she get? Feeling whipped, she wiped a tear.

Moments later, she glanced down to the tattered, worn, leather Bible laying on the seat beside her.

"What do I do now?" she asked her traveling companions, Matthew, Mark, Luke, and John. "Am I defeated?" Humility had now replaced her anger.

Her fight gone, she paid little attention when her foot slipped off the brake. The truck crept down the incline with a will of it's own. At the bottom of Powder Mill Hill, she glanced out the window and saw the outdoor display of crafts. She braked, turned in, and parked. Why? She couldn't have told you. She lived less than eight miles from this business, traveled by it often, yet, she couldn't recall ever visiting the place.

Minutes passed before she made a move to open the truck door. However, when she stepped inside the craft shop, her problems were put on a back burner. She was awed by the stunning array of different craft items, and beautiful hand-made quilts.

"Can I help you?"

She turned, unaware that she was rudely staring at the tall, good-looking man. She was thinking a real frontiersman. A frontiersman that fit the elements. She hastily glanced around the inside of the high, rustic looking building. And still captured by thoughts, she turned slightly and stared

Barbara Howell and Todd Yannayon.

out the undressed window. Tears filled her eyes as she watched the rainbow colors dancing up and down the tumbling waterfall at the beck of the sun.

She sniffed the perfume smell of the soap and candles as it permeated the air. The smell of hickory wood burning in the pot-bellied stove stirred her childhood memories. This man and his crafts were pure country. The country atmosphere, bathed and revived her as water to desert-chapped lips.

"Can I help you?" the mountain-looking man repeated, seeing he had her attention this time.

"Do you know of a place in Huntland where you can buy wood?" she asked, telling him of her relationship with the Amish.

"Tennessee Valley Wood?" he asked.

"Probably," she murmured, praying her ignorance didn't show, but inwardly aware that the name didn't strike a memory.

He immediately began giving her directions. "Please, could you draw me a map," she interrupted, and added, "I ain't too good with this driving business and direction thing."

He showed no arrogance and did as she asked. Not only that, he walked her through the map pointing out certain details even down to the auto parts house nearby, and cautioned her to be sure and turn above this business.

She thanked him and clutched the map in her hand. "Be sure to stay on Highway 64, and you can't get lost," he called out, smiling, when she turned and gave him a salute.

She found Tennessee Valley Wood that day, and some great guys as well. She is still doing business with them today.

Barbara will tell you that she believes in divine guidance. Her first meeting with Todd Yannayon was over 10 years ago. Yet, that meeting is as fresh in her mind as if it happened yesterday. And you can't imagine her shock upon learning years later, that Todd was a former Mennonite. She believes strongly that he was hand-picked by her Heavenly Guidance to help her that day.

Todd's last words, "Stay on Highway 64 and you can't get lost," were stamped on her mind. She followed his directions to the letter. For two whole years, she hogged the highway, weaving trailer loads of wood right smack through the middle of the adjoining town to Huntland, Tennessee. She was so focused on Highway 64 that she paid no attention to the horn blowing, and angry cursing of the impatient drivers who frantically waved her toward the alternate truck route.

The crocheted Toy Clown that blazed the trail to crafts shows that eventually led to shows and travel across the United States.

Recipe swapping, lap quilting, and crocheting disclosed the times. It was the mid-80s. Barbara's Beauty Shop buzzed with activity. And true to the profession, ladies who patronized the business could catch up on the latest news and gossip of their small southern town, located 79 miles south of Nashville, Tennessee.

These ladies were not just paying customers, they were good friends; some since school days. They shared stories of their families, and were often involved in the lives of each other's children and grandchildren.

Several of the older ladies had adopted Barbara's daughter, Jeannea, as their own. Jeannea was a stay-at-home mom except for doing substitute teaching at the local high school. Barbara and her customers always baby-sat while Jeannea was working. The grandchildren didn't mind. They loved the ladies. And their granny, Barbara, had a special table reserved just for them, loaded with goodies. Barbara's Beauty Shop was a fun place for all.

Jeannea returned to the beauty shop one afternoon after work to pick up her children. When she stepped through the door, she spied "Granny" Birdie Alford sitting under the hair dryer, crocheting. Jeannea's eyes took on a sparkle. She had been trying to learn this art with little success. She suspected if she hung around she could get a free lesson in crocheting.

She never dreamed that this seemingly little insignificant whim, that she satisfied that day with Granny Alford as her teacher, would eventually blaze out future trails for the whole Howell family. But it did. And it happened in this fashion. A few days later when called into work, Jeannea dropped her girls off at their favorite place, each clinging to their newly crocheted clown.

The multicolored clown did not go unnoticed, or have a clue to its future. So soft and lovable, arrayed in striking colors, the crocheted toy clown made a terrific hit among the ladies who patronized the beauty shop. Soon they were putting in orders for the toy clown in their favorite colors to give to their children or grandchildren, for birthdays and Christmas.

A few weeks later, due to an appointment swap, Helen Lantz, a good friend and weekly patron, was in the shop and saw the toy clown. Her interest was sparked. Helen was involved in arts and crafts shows, having learned how to use her talents to make money. Soon, she had Barbara and her daughter, Jeannea, booked in an upcoming arts and crafts show at the New Prospect Community Center.

They made $50 dollars. They thought they had a landslide. They were hooked.

"Hey, Jeannea! You know this little stepstool of Jen's? Wouldn't that be a perfect item to sell with your crocheted toy clown at the craft fairs?" Barbara yelled from the bathroom one afternoon. She reached down and picked up the stool that had little feet painted on it. Her pride began to glow as she ran her fingers across Jennifer's name written on the top step.

Where it all began! Barbara's beauty shop was inspected and graded on a regular basis. Also, she had to go before and pass a governing Tennessee State Board in Nashville, Tennessee to get her Cosmetologist License, and not only that, she had to keep them renewed on a yearly basis.

"You got it!" Jeannea squealed in excitement, running down the hallway. But reality struck just as she poked her head inside the bathroom where her mom was standing, holding the little step-stool.

"Mom, I can't drag my babies out to some craft fair every weekend. They deserve better than this." Her face became capped in sadness, aware of the financial cost this sacrifice brought.

"Me and your daddy can do the traveling and selling until the children get bigger," Barbara volunteered with enthusiasm.

"I know daddy wouldn't mind, but can you handle the beauty shop and the crafts shows? I'm sure Kenny and I can make the crafts," Jeannea said, referring to her husband.

"Sure, I can," Barbara spoke with more confidence than she felt.

And true to their character, Barbara and Charles got right into the project. Soon they were investing money in the business just like it was their own. They bought patterns for the sewing side, as well as wood patterns, and never took one penny for anything.

Financially, things were looking up for the kids, and in just a matter of months Jeannea resigned her teaching position.

They booked several crafts shows, and a friend helped them get into the Nashville Flea Market. This was a big achievement. The Nashville Flea Market was, and still is, a very strong selling market. Barbara began toying with the idea of selling her beauty shop business.

Copperas Branch reunion planned

by Sandi Mashburn

The annual Copperas Branch School Reunion is fast approaching, and all former teachers, students, families and friends are invited to attend.

The Copperas Branch Community Club meets inside the old Copperas Branch School building, a one-room structure erected by members of the community and the Lawrence County Board of Education in 1929. According to club officials, Copperas Branch is the only one-room school house in the county that is still being used.

According to a history of the school compiled by Cathy Mize in 1996, the school board approved a school for Copperas Branch, then purchased one acre of land and use of an existing well from Mr. and Mrs. R.W. Lantz for the sum of one dollar. Lumber and labor were provided by members of the community, and a high-priced carpenter was hired at a wage of 30¢ an hour, to oversee the project.

Completed in the spring of 1929, grades one through eight were taught within the confines of the one-room school house. The building served the community's educational needs until the school board consolidated the community schools in 1953.

After standing empty at the mercy of vandals for three years, in February of 1957 the community opted to purchase the building and grounds for the purchase price of $300 and form the Copperas Branch Community Club.

One of the club's many community projects has been hosting the annual school reunion. During this year's event, nine individuals will be honored who formerly served as teachers at the school. Honorees include:

*Lorene White Brown who taught at the school 2 ½ months between 1928 and 1929
*Jennie Frazier Kelton who taught 1929-1931 and 1933-1936
*Orville Quillen who taught from 1931 to 1933
*Eva Henderson Prince who taught from 1936-1945
*Trula Fox Copeland who served as a substitute teacher in 1943
*Viva Lee Hendrix Peppers who served as a substitute teacher in 1943
*Alba Quillen Franks who taught from 1945-1950
*Ona Nix who taught from 1950-1952
*Elizabeth Smith Clark who taught from 1952-1953

Everyone is invited to attend the year 2000 Copperas Branch School Reunion scheduled to get underway at 10:00 a.m. on Saturday, September 9.

L. (White) Brown

J. (Frazier) Kelton

O. Quillen

Eva (Henderson) Prince

Trula (Fox) Copeland

Alba (Quillen) Franks

Ona Nix

Elizabeth Smith Clark

Barbara's first, third, and fourth grade teacher.

Barbara's fifth and sixth grade teacher.

Barbara's seventh grade teacher.

Four years had past. Barbara was still doing craft shows for the children, and keeping her hairdressing business afloat. She flirted often with the idea of hanging up her comb and scissors, tempted the most when pain between her shoulders would get so severe she couldn't raise her arms for days. Still, fear kept her to the grindstone. Financial fear? No. They were comfortable. What then? Her mind could never pin it down.

Then, one day, pushed to the edge by pain, she made a phone call. The sale of her business was finalized without a hitch. Sold. Sadness torched her heart and brought gloom. She couldn't shake the feeling that her financial future was doomed.

"Could she?" The inward question shuffled scenes before her eyes. Scenes of an old dream she had secretly stashed on the imaginary shelf in her mind. "Could she?" The question demanded an answer now, pestering her in silent accusation.

Her mind grew restless, haunted by her cowardice. One day she decided to *just do it!* She did. She promptly picked up the phone, and enrolled in a college night class at the local high school.

"You can't do this!" Fear grabbed her and a vivid imagination tightened her enemy's grip.

Barbara is deaf in one ear, and has only 30 percent hearing in the other. Nerves were permanently damaged by high fever from childhood diseases. It isn't just a matter of not being able to hear. Her other senses are affected, such as sense of direction, walking, and balance. Now, although she hadn't admitted it, age had become another enemy strengthening her handicap.

"I can do it," she argued her unseen enemy aloud. "I know I can do it."

Her argumentative thoughts suddenly hitched a ride down memory lane. Plain as day, she saw the little one-room school house where she had attended her first six years of school. Her teacher's faces sped before her eyes. Her bravery surged, when in imagination, she cast herself into their shoes. They each had chosen the challenge of manning, all alone, eight grades in this little country school located in the backwoods of Tennessee. Their call indisputable, they had prevailed.

She fixed her memory on her seventh grade report card. It was all A's. A satisfied smirk settled her face. She knew that neither her teachers nor fellow students had suspected her handicap. What if they had? What could they have done? Nothing! This was the early 1940s, Hitler and his war dominated the lives of even this small rural community of Copperas Branch.

Barbara learned body language, lip reading, and developed a sixth sense. She graduated from Lawrence County High School in 1958. In 1972, she graduated from cosmetology college. Again, aware, that neither the instructor, nor fellow students had a clue to her hearing loss.

The ink barely dry on her diploma, she built a very successful hair dressing business under the umbrella of her home. It wasn't until later years that her family began to suspect she needed to see a doctor for her hearing problem.

A doctor at Vanderbilt Hospital in Nashville, Tennessee was both awed and appalled. "Why didn't

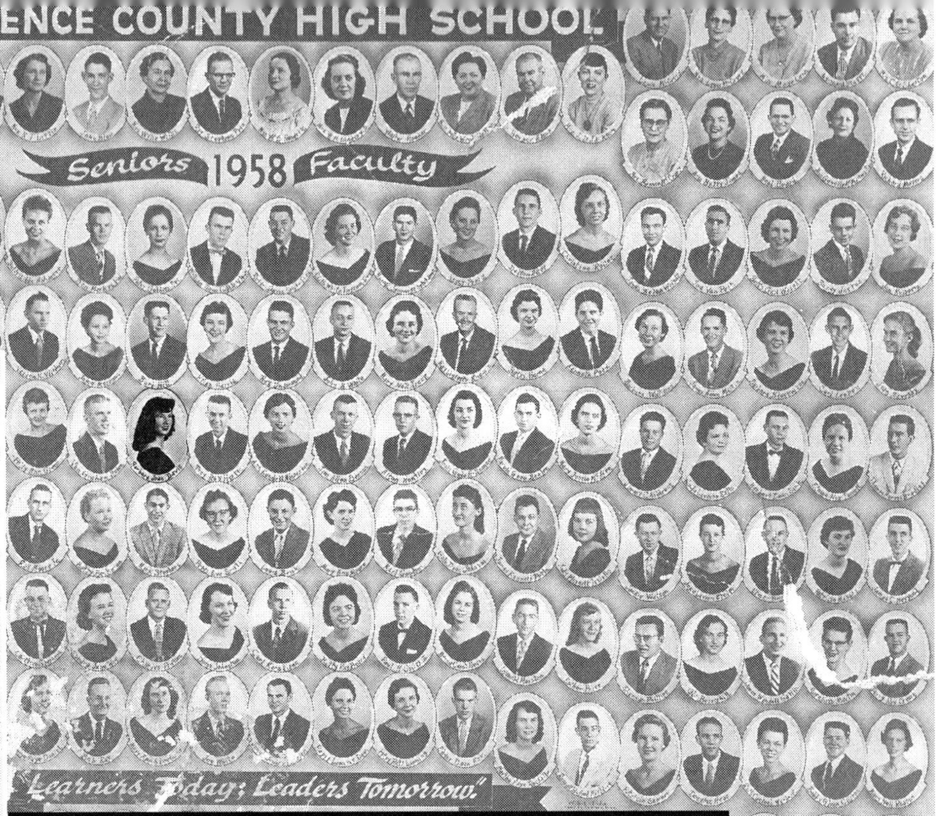

Barbara's high school graduation. See! No glasses.

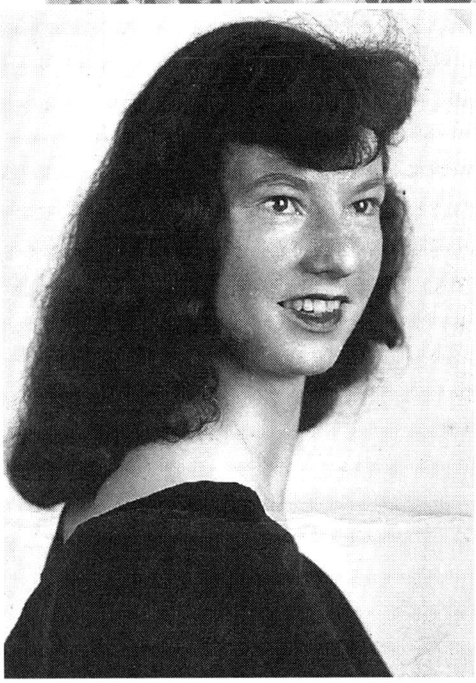

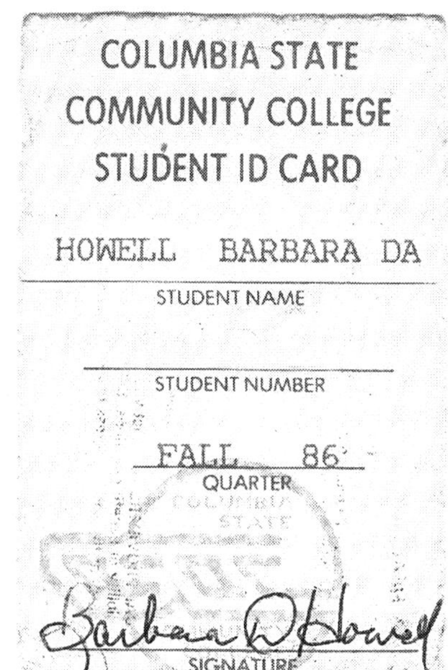

your parents seek medical attention?" Barbara didn't miss the doctor's tone of condemnation.

"We just weren't taken to doctors," Barbara answered, somewhat defensively.

"How did you cope in school? How do you keep your balance? Nerve loss of this severity almost always affects balance." Barbara showed no offense now at the doctor's questions, for she could see genuine concern in the physician's eyes.

"The Good Lord helps me," Barbara grinned, somewhat relieved that the doctor had unintentionally explained her tendency for poor balance, which had often resulted in broken bones and sprained ankles.

"Somebody sure helps you," the lady doctor acknowledged, her animosity gone now.

Barbara is a fighter by nature. She was raised by a grandfather who taught her never start a fight, but never run from one. And if pushed, go down swinging. Her grandfather's psychology had served her well in fighting her handicap. She was no whiner and no quitter.

COLUMBIA STATE
COMMUNITY COLLEGE
STUDENT ID CARD

HOWELL BARBARA DA
STUDENT NAME

STUDENT NUMBER

FALL 86
QUARTER

Barbara D Howell
SIGNATURE
F-51A

Her mind slowly drifted back to the present, and she was no longer afraid. She had perfect assurance she would find a way to cope. Heck, she just might get serious about this college thing, someday. This thought put a smug smile on her face and a spring in her step.

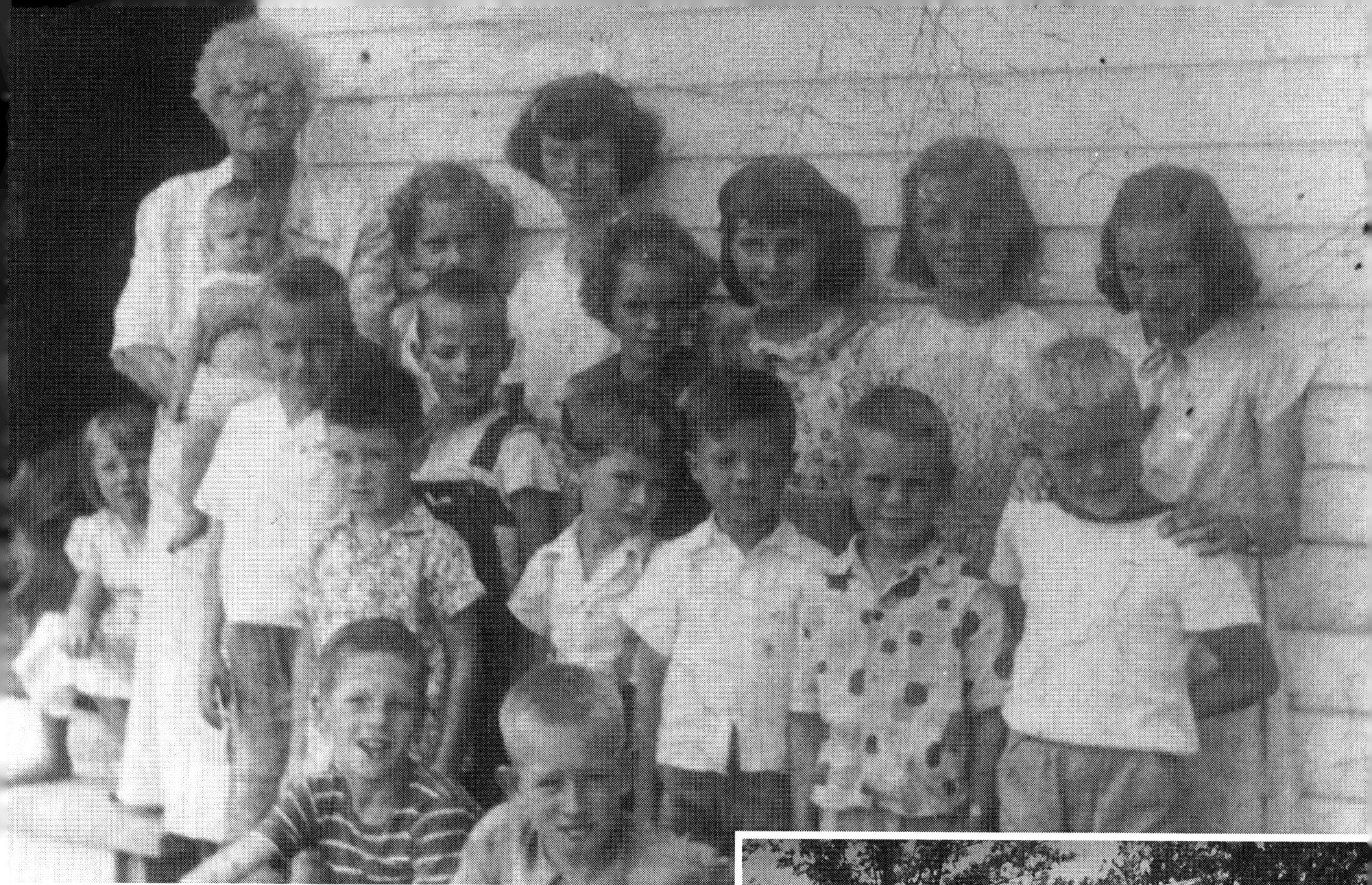

Copperas Branch School Kids.

First row left to right: Paul Price, Jack Hill **Second row:** Bryon Robinson, Bobby Smith, Jerry Price, Eddie Dewberry and Travis Clark. **Third row:** Sammy Price, Robert Davis, Carolyn Clark. **Fourth Row:** Irene Price, (peeking around the teacher) the teacher, Mrs. Ona Nix, Eunice Price's baby in teacher's arms, Leda Faye Prince, Barbara (Davis) Howell, Lula Ann Curtis, Barbara Price, Imogene Smith.

Above: As you can see, we were a very laid back and a happy group of kids at our beloved Copperas Branch School. We took out from our class work and had our picture made. The teacher is Mrs. Ona Nix. The way I remember it: The baby, the teacher is holding belonged to the older sister of several of the students—The Price children. I remember their sister being married and coming back for a visit. Little Irene Price, peeking around the teacher is probably four or five years old. And her big sister, Eunice is taking the picture.

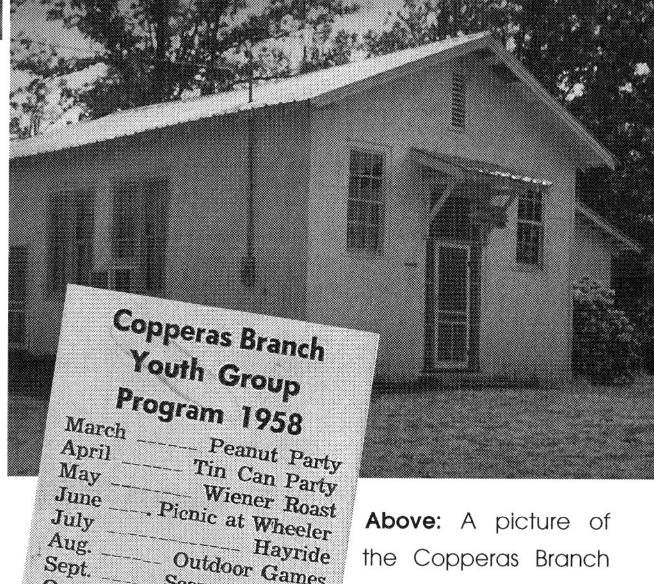

Above: A picture of the Copperas Branch Schoolhouse as it stands today. (2008)

Copperas Branch Youth Group Program 1958

March ------ Peanut Party
April ------ Tin Can Party
May ------ Wiener Roast
June ---- Picnic at Wheeler
July ------ Hayride
Aug. ------ Outdoor Games
Sept. ------ Scavanger Hunt
Oct. ------ Tacky Party
Nov. ------ Open
Dec. ------ Christmas Party

Officers For 1958

President -- Buddy Howell
Vice-Pres. -- Charles Owens
Sec.-Treas. -- Dot Williams
Song Leader -- Syble Sides
Reporter --- Barbara Davis

Right: When the Copperas Branch community bought the old school house they formed a Copperas Branch Youth Group Program at the school house for all the teenagers in the community. Certain ladies of the community helped with the chaperoning of Barbara and her friends: Beulah Prince, Mary Prince McDougal, Bessie Smith, Mildred Davis, Mattie Prince, Pearl Smith, Marie Owens and Eula Williams. This was a huge success and provided good, clean fun for the teenagers, as well as, the Summer, Sunday Evening soft ball games directed by Mr. Harlie Sides.

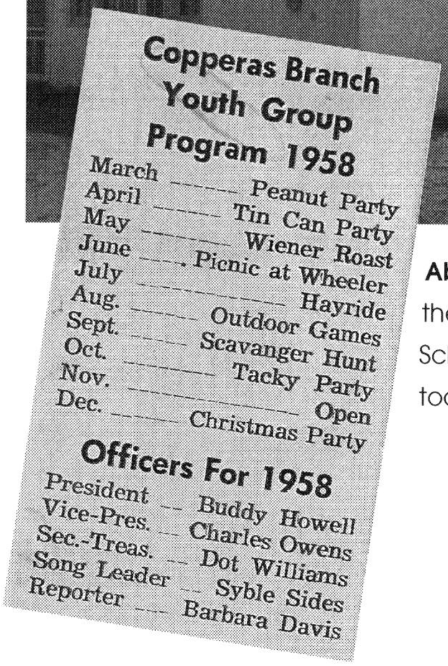

teachers that shaped a young life

Mrs. Alba (Quillen) Franks

Alba (Quillen) Franks

I started at Copperas Branch School in 1947. I was almost seven years old. I was held back by my mom in order to start with my brother who was one year younger. Mrs. Alba (Quillen) Franks was my first teacher, and the first, and only teacher, that gave me a paddling. I don't remember why, but I said she was crazy. I didn't tell her this to her face, but her grandson (Alex) heard me say it, and told on me. When confronted, I wouldn't deny it. (Thank God! Back then, we were taught not to say ugly things behind our teacher's back.) I skipped the second grade and was promoted to the third grade at the end of the year. Mom's plan to keep us together failed, despite her keeping me back a year, for my little brother only passed to the second grade, therefore, we were separated the rest of our school days.

Mrs. Ona Nix

Ona Nix

Mrs. Ona Nix was my teacher from 1950 through 1952. She was a great teacher, and I loved her very much. She was a fine Christian lady and believed in good works. One Thanksgiving, she got together with someone, (I never knew who) and they fixed Thanksgiving boxes for the poor folks in our community. When someone knocked on our door that night, mother answered the door and was presented a big Thanksgiving box of food, and other goodies. When I realized what was conspiring, I jumped up and jerked the box from mother's hand and was fixing to fling it out the door behind the good Christian lady, and was being backed all the way by my granddaddy. We weren't poor! We didn't accept charity! We worked! The only thing that saved the pride of that good woman was my mama's begging and crying, for mother was very tender hearted and didn't ever want to hurt anyone's feelings. The next day, we had our regular Thanksgiving dinner, (a king's feast), for my granddaddy always prided himself for setting a fine table, as he called it, and not the first thing was touched from that good woman's gift box. And it was many years before I came to appreciate, and understand what that fine Christian lady's motive was on that eve before Thanksgiving. You see, my mama was a single mother before it became fashionable. This teacher didn't know that my granddaddy was a well respected man of the community and had given up a good job connected with the army in Tullahoma to come back to his farm to help raise his grandchildren when my daddy and mother separated. And my grandfather had his ways of letting people know his grandchildren weren't poor nor neglected. We never received anymore charitable Thanksgiving boxes.

Elizabeth Smith Clark

Elizabeth Smith Clark was my seventh grade teacher. She was my favorite! She was very young and beautiful. She only got to teach one year at our beloved Copperas Branch School. They consolidated our school and we were bused to New Prospect School. My eighth grade year was a nightmare. This was my baby sister's first year in school. She wanted no part of a bus or a big school. And upon being forced to go to school every morning, in just a matter of hours, she wound up in my class. By the time she got there, she was in such an emotional state of turmoil from being made to stay in her class, I usually had to take her home. She disrupted my class, embarrassed me, and sent her first grade teacher around the bend. And this went on for weeks. Every day! Finally to solve our problem, my mom talked my baby brother into going back into the first grade from the third grade to be with her. This solved my problem, however, by this time, my grades and my reputation were totally wrecked, or so I thought. I can still remember the shock that struck my new teacher's face when I handed him my seventh grade report card. It was all A's. Here, I was barely passing his class, and in his hands was a report card that said, I was a straight A student. Shock! Shock! Don't judge a book by its cover. The emotional trauma of being bused to another school, and the ordeal of my baby sister's problem left its mark, I didn't totally recover and get a handle on my grades until my high school years.

Barbara standing beside the Greyhound bus
in the Windy City. Chicago, Illinois, 1960.

The year was 1960. Summer was in full bloom. Barbara stepped away from the greyhound bus in Chicago, Illinois anticipating a long lay over. She and her uncle had been riding for hours. They were on their way to Rockford, Illinois to see family. She was tired and nervous as she made her way to the coffee shop.

"Ya'll got any coffee here?" Barbara butchered the English language, eyeing the man behind the counter.

"Say that again," the young man smiled, making no move to get her coffee.

At first, puzzled by his request, unaware he was enjoying her southern slang, she didn't obey.

"Say that again. I want to hear you say that again," he repeated himself, his stance relaying to her he wasn't moving until she obeyed.

"Ya'll got any coffee here?" she spoke louder, embarrassed by his attention.

"Where do you live?" he asked, still making no move to serve her.

"I live in Tennessee. Now can I get my cotton-pickin' coffee?" she snapped, pointing to the coffee maker.

He roared in laughter and made no move until it struck him, she was holding up the line. He turned slowly, aware her angry eyes bored holes in his back.

Barbara hastily flung a nickel down on the counter and hissed, "Smart ass." She saw his flinch and got her rush. She whirled around and made a quick escape from the coffee shop.

Thirty years later, enrolled at the University of North Alabama, studying creative writing, Barbara was still butchering the English language. She was often asked to repeat this and that. Now older and wiser, she no longer got offended and was learning how to use this art to her advantage in writing.

The night classes she had attended at the little community college in her hometown had whet her appetite and spurred her on to get more knowledge. Stuffing her pride and independence, she had asked her husband if he would take her to the college for evening classes. He had agreed and she was finding the creative writing classes super.

She was meeting famous writers. She was hearing about their failures as well as their successes. Their suggestions of certain books, *The Synonym Finder* and *Webster's Rhyming Dictionary* were gold mines. Tools, that all writers needed, she was told by the professionals.

The pinnacle of joy for all the would-be-writers in her class was, The Writer's Conference, hosted by the university once a year. It was the talk of the class, and proved to be everything Barbara had heard. She met agents from New York, who gave her helpful tips on how to judge an agency to

critique her work without being fleeced.

Her fears were all behind her. Then it happened! She was introduced to the computer. Nothing in her past had prepared her for this enemy. She hated it on sight. She battled the computer with venom surging through her veins. It gave no mercy. It stole her whole day of beautiful words in one heart-beat of forgetfulness, or one power blink.

Her son's dogged persistence, and the fact that he took her Underwood Typewriter when he set up this new monster, had forced her into this fight. He had paid no attention to her excuses for not wanting to learn computer. He came home from South Carolina and set up a whole computer system for her.

He assured her he was only a phone call away, never admitting, but probably wishing, he had

left her alone. She called him every day! Sometimes 10 times a day. But finally, she mastered the monster.

In time, a New York agency accepted some of her work, critiquing it with encouragement. She knew she was almost there. Then, once again, her dream was shelved by a family crisis, and her walk toward hell began.

put up
or shut up

Barbara had gotten serious about this writing business– proof follows.

Despite my dreams being aborted once again, in later years, I came to realize nothing in my back-to-school years had been wasted. I had accomplished something that kept the secret flame burning in my heart while on my short journey through Columbia State Community College in 1986, at age 46 and my short stay at the University of North Alabama at age 50.

My *Creative Writing* teacher at the University of North Alabama had just recently been published when we started our classes in 1990. She related how she reached a point of telling herself, "PUT UP OR SHUT UP!"

This one statement challenged me to look inside myself and ask, *Did I want truth?* The truth of knowing whether I had the ability with words to grab attention, stir passions, and opinions.

I overheard another writing teacher say, "Students, you have 30 seconds or less to grab your reader's attention. Novice writers often pick controversial topics such as religion or politics to break into their field of expertise. For upcoming reporters, writers, and wannabes, getting their first article in

(continued on next page)

LAWRENCE COUNTY ADVOCATE, WEDNESDAY, JANUARY 30, 1991, PAGE A-4

ADVOCATE EDITORIALS

Reader says: "Our hero is the patriot missile"

To the Editor:

WAR! The splatter of blood, screaming sirens, a scramble for shelters, these are just some of the tentacles of war.

Sane people will all agree, war is hell but sometimes necessary.

It boasts of separating the men from the boys, and the making of heroes. And thus far, the gulf war has proved to be no exception. Our hero - the patriot missile, which has saved countless lives and prevented untold injuries.

However, when this is all over, will the real hero, or heroes, be awarded a medal and a lesson learned? Probably not, for we are proned to forget the sweat, guts and pain that goes into making a hero.

America, as you sleep a little more peaceful tonight in regard to our love ones in the Persian Gulf, let's pause and be thankful for our unsung heroes considering the birth of this patriot missile - President Reagan and others, who had to battle senators, congressmen, and a host of grumbling Americans, myself included, for his outrageous spending on Star Wars.

When the dust of this war has settled, again, there will be sacrifices to be made.

Will we then remember the birth of our hero? Or will our creature comforts and selfishness rear its ugly head? Can we be counted on to vote issues or party? Or will we in our humanness of forgetfulness take a leaf from my granddaddy's book - in his loyalty to his party, he always said, "My candidate may be a son-of-a-bitch but he's a Republican!"

Barbara Howell

TimesDaily, Sunday, February 24, 1991   11A

Sacrifices to be made

To the editor:

Sane people will all agree war is hell but sometimes necessary.

It boasts of separating the men from the boys, and the making of heroes. And thus far, the gulf war has proved to be no exception.

Our hero? The patriot missile, which has saved countless lives and prevented untold injuries.

However, when this is all over, will the real hero, or heroes, be awarded a medal and a lesson learned? Probably not, for we are prone to forget the sweat, guts, and pain that goes into the making of a national hero.

America, as you can sleep a little more peaceful tonight in regard to our loved ones in the Persian Gulf, let's pause and consider the birth of this patriot missile — President Reagan and others, who had to battle senators, congressmen, and a host of grumbling Americans, myself included, for his outrageous spending on Star Wars.

When the dust of this war has settled, again, there will be sacrifices to be made.

Will we then remember the birth of our hero? Or will our creature's comforts and selfishness rear its ugly head? Can we be counted on to vote issues or party?

BARBARA HOWELL
Lawrenceburg, Tenn.

Reader says: We should "love rainbows more than Rambo's"

To the Editor:

"God, Guns and Guts" was scrawled on a banner being waved at a recent pro-war demonstration. The moral confusion of those who believe that these three concepts go together is appalling. It's bad enough that we're involved in a war for all the wrong reasons- losing and taking precious human lives, but to self-righteously justify this by assuming that God is on "our side" is pure idolatry. I imagine God weeps over the power brokers of this world and with those who suffer at their hands.

To glorify weapons of death and their usage as something heroic and laudable is not the same as the glorification of God. Over and over we misunderstand the nature of the Kingdom of God. It is not about power over others but power from within which radically changes our values. Don't we teach our children that God is love, our strength, our defense and our refuge?

A letter appeared here last week singing the praises of our "heroes" the patriot missiles, and the people who had them built. The writer said we sleep "a little more peaceful" at night because of the birth of this new savior of "countless lives, untold injuries". She says we should "remember the birth of our hero" when the dust of this war has settled" because "there will be sacrifices to be made." "Outrageous spending" is necessary to buy our freedom, our security. What we are doing is bowing and paying homage to a false god, who gives us in return only enslavement and a false sense of security.

All of our tremendous arsenals cannot protect us from the spiritual rotting that is going on at the core of our supposedly Christian nation. We are honoring the wrong things, misplacing our allegiance and our priorities.

Our national defense must begin with pledging allegiance to honor the life of each and every one of God's children everywhere. The only real security lies in beating swords into plowshares, in putting our talents, energy and love into ending the massive problems that stem from hunger and poverty. What the world spends on weapons in three weeks time - would feed, clothe and house every human being on the planet.

A Children's Defense Fund poster contains this quote by Dwight D. Eisenhower:

"Every gun that is made, every rocket fired signifies. . . a theft from those who hunger and are not fed, those who are cold and are not clothed. This world in arms is not spending money alone. It is spending the sweat of its laborers, the genius of its scientists, the hope of its children."

If we are to be saved we must, as a people, begin to place God before Caesar, life before death. We must show our true grit - end our sick fascination with violence and love rainbows more than Rambos. What wonderful things would happen if people let go of their fears, their pride and their need for idols so that God's peace could be born on earth as it is in heaven.

Shalom,
Diane Saliba

print is no small accomplishment. To get the same article published in two different publications shows a gift for writing. To get feedback and your contents specifically mentioned in a positive or negative fashion shows you have an ability to stir people's passions and opinions and will certainly earn you an A in my class."

The "No-No Principle" suddenly flashed my mind. I realized the "No-No Principle" in one profession, could be a strength in another profession.

In explaination, while I was in Cosmetology College, I was taught to avoid certain subjects such as religion and politics. At UNA in our writing classes we were taught that controversial subjects grabs attention and stirs passions.

PUT UP OR SHUT UP! I decided to put out a Gideon fleece. Here is a copy of my efforts, and as you can see, I would have gotten an A in one teacher's class. I don't remember the grade I got in my class. Ha!

Charlie and his showcases. He took great pride in his work. His most unusual piece was
the case for a Huntsville, Alabama man to display a piece of the Berlin Wall.

It was early May of 1988. Barbara looked up from the book as her husband came into the room. "Hey!" she smiled.

Charlie grunted and dropped into the nearest chair, spraying sawdust.

"Charlie, why don't you dust yourself off in the shop instead of bringing all that sawdust upstairs?" she scolded, getting up to dust him.

"I have to work, Saturday. And I've heard some rumors that this may not be the only one," he growled, pushing her away, dusting himself.

Seeing his foul mood, she hurriedly made her escape to the kitchen.

"Did you hear what I said about working Saturday?" he asked, dogging her steps.

"Aye aye, Admiral!" she saluted, deliberately scratching his itch for a fight, her hopes dashed of avoiding a confrontation.

"I'm in no mood for a smart ass," he said. "Instead of playing nanny, you are going to sell my showcases this weekend at the flea market. And you are going to start helping me some in the shop. You can put screws in the sides, and I think you could put on some backs."

He turned to leave and snarled back over his shoulder, "And I don't want none of your back-talk. Not tonight."

"But you don't always get what you want, do you, Admiral?" she whirled around in a huff, only to see he had left the room.

How dare he! She fumed. And in seconds, she was lathered up for a cat and dog fight.

She marched into the living room where he sat. She glared down at him and said, "Charlie, I know nothing about a drill. I'm not a carpenter, and I don't have any intentions of ever being one."

He stared up at her, his eyes speaking volumes. Then maliciously, he took a sarcastic bow.

Barbara knew him. She had bedded the subject tonight. But her flat refusal to cooperate had escalated the war. She knew there would be hell to pay. But right now, in her fit of temper, she didn't care.

Weeks later, their relationship was still strained as he pouted. One night, alone in the kitchen, she rinsed the supper dishes for the dishwasher. Her mind wandered back to the beginning of his showcase business.

One day just out of the blue, Charlie said, "Fred hinted to me last month that he was going to quit the flea market in December."

"So?" Barbara asked, her interest sparked.

"So, I've been thinking," he paused, getting so lost in thought that he missed her mischievous grin as she fought the temptation to wise-crack his thinking power. However, soon his hesitation pushed her to the limit of patience, and she said, "You've been thinking what?"

"Fred said he would give me some glass."

"Fred said he would give you some glass," she repeated in monotone.

"Yeah."

She waited. And waited. Still, he gave no explanation. She hated this personality quirk with a passion, knowing he wanted her to fish, which she did, as always, unable to wait him out.

"Are you talking about the old man that sets up in the corner booth close to us at the Nashville Flea Market?" she strained to hide her aggravation.

"Yes, that's Fred. He makes them show boxes."

"That's Fred huh?" She mocked him in open defiance now.

"I think I could do it," he said, her mockery going right over his head. "What I mean is, I think I could make boxes like Fred's. What do you think?"

"Oh, definitely," she said, her mood quickly shifting away from any show of arrogance now. "You have the gift for wood working. But have you thought all this through?"

"Well, you know your beauty shop now is just sitting there empty. And we are at the shows every weekend for the kids. Why not start making a little money on the side for us. But, I don't know where I would get the wood. Or the hardware. And besides, I know the saws and equipment would cost a lot of money." She saw he was back-pedaling.

"You could start off small," she suggested, trying not to push. "Take baby steps like we did with the beauty shop business,"

"Well, I know the selling part wouldn't be hard," he said, his defeated attitude somewhat shifting. "We are already established in crafts shows and flea markets selling for Jeannea."

"Well, maybe Fred could help you out with some information. I know he can't help with the wood issue because he lives in Kentucky." She saw his frown and quickly zipped her lips.

A few days later, with much surprise, she watched Charlie take some steps toward fulfilling his dream. In less than a month, her abandoned beauty shop had sprung to life. It was no longer the sing of hair dryers and the chatter of women. Instead, it was the buzzing sounds of power saws, drill presses, and sanders that were making melody in the air.

And true to form, Charles wasn't far into his project before he showed his possessive streak. He informed Jeannea and her husband he would sell his own crafts, but they had to sell theirs. But, he did make one concession–he told them he would share a booth.

This was fine with them. The children were older, and they would have granny as their overseer.

It worked.

But nothing works forever! Barbara moodily shifted her thinking back to the present. Her fears had materialized. Charlie had been informed today that the plant where he was a welder had scheduled the next six Saturdays to work, beginning with the upcoming Saturday.

He had told her his bad news, loaded for bear by telling her plainly, "Your nanny business is closed. You are going to sell my showcases this weekend at the flea market. And that isn't all. You are going to help me with this business, starting tomorrow night."

This time, Barbara accepted her fate without argument.

A few nights later, Charlie jerked the drill from her hand and snapped, "You can't be that dumb! Do you know what you have done? You have just buried five dollars worth of drill bits in one side of a display case."

"I didn't know the bits were that expensive," she shot back in defense. "I told you I can't hold that dang drill, it's too heavy."

"You can't run the drill! You can't sell the showcases! You don't know one case from another. I give up, Barbara. You won't ever become a carpenter's helper, much less a carpenter," he sneered, as he went for the juggler.

Soon a slinging match got into full swing. When the dust had settled, Barbara suggested calmly, "Well, if you would mark the cases for me I think I could learn a matchbox from a shot glass, a 1/24 scale from a 1/18 scale. I can't make the dang things. But I know I could learn to sell them if you would take time to teach me one from another!" She had managed to get the last word with dignity.

She glanced at him and quickly read his expression he was trying so hard to hide. He knew she had a point. But, not yet ready to admit it, he growled, "The dad-blame cases wouldn't have to be marked if you'd learn how to count squares."

It took money walking off to overcome his stubbornness. He finally began to mark the cases. And it helped tremendously. But it had no bearing on her knowing oak from cherry, or maple from poplar, but in her favor, she could identify the black walnut wood. Of course, he seldom made black walnut cases.

Swamped with overtime at the plant and an abundance of case orders, Charlie had little time for anything but work. Barbara nagged him constantly about his neglect of the family and Bible reading. He paid her no mind, and when the phone call came that fatal night, he was totally unprepared.

"Charlie, your mom is on the phone," Barbara bellowed from upstairs. She had hoped to get his attention without having to trudge down the stairway that led to his work shop.

It didn't happen. "Hang on, and I'll go fetch him," Barbara laid the phone down and moved toward the stairway.

She had already taken a couple of steps back up the stairs when she heard her husband say, "Hello?"

Suddenly, she stopped in mid-stride hearing Charlie yell, "What the hell is Bobby doing in jail?"

For seconds she didn't hear a peep. She pivoted and tiptoed back down the stairs, eavesdropping on the conversation, curious as to why her brother-in-law was in jail.

"Mom, there is not one damn thing that I can do tonight to get Bobby out of jail!"

Undetected, Barbara strained to hear every word.

Moments later, she watched as he angrily slapped the wall phone against its cradle.

"Hey Charlie, calm down. Bobby is like a cat, he has nine lives." Barbara moved slowly away from the stairs toward Charlie, letting her presence become known.

"Number nine has just come up," Charlie snapped, jerking around, startled by her presence.

"What do you mean?" she asked, more somber now.

"Bobby has been arrested for arson and charged with six murders. And worse, he will be tried with the death penalty."

"The nursing home?" she said slowly.

"Right," he answered, as he dropped down on the bottom stair step, slumping in defeat.

This picture stands as a symbol, of both good and bad. It brought justice to six families, and helped to destroy four families, when they chose to walk in the denial of truth.

his brother's keeper

Barbara and Charlie got involved with his brother's costly defense mainly because of his mom.

If asked, they would have been truthful and admitted the man probably owed the state some time for arson. For despite family ties, it was unbelievable, even for them, that someone could have had 14 accidental fires on personal properties. Yes. 14. This was the count that Charlie and another brother came up with one night after the arrest. They heard about fires they previously had no knowledge of.

However, upon learning how this crime had "supposedly" taken place as told by some of the prosecution's witnesses, they were plagued with doubt concerning his brother's guilt.

Still, mom was the real issue. She had tottered for years on the edge, suffering from mental illness. And now with age, her physical health had deteriorated severely as well. She had to have some help and encouragement with this burden. This boy jailed, was hers. In fact her favorite son.

Charlie and Barbara found they couldn't ignore her pain and live with themselves.

The trial proved to be long and costly. Barbara and Charlie did most of the leg work, hiring and meeting with lawyers. Along with another brother, they had shared the bigger part of the expenses, which, when all totaled, was almost $40,000.

Barbara worked with the defense lawyers. She was at the court house from day one of jury selection while her husband worked his factory job. When all was said and done, and the dust had settled, Bobby was found guilty of aggravated arson, and six counts of second-degree murder. The trial court sentenced Bobby to a life sentence in each of the second-degree murder conviction to run consecutively, and a sentence of 35 years in the aggravated arson case to run concurrent with one of the second-degree murder convictions.

Figuratively speaking, Charlie and Barbara began serving his time, for Bobby constantly whined for Charlie to do something to get him out of prison.

In time, his whining turned to blame and meanness. He blamed Charlie. He blamed his lawyers. He began to make threats of suing them all. His beef was no one had worked hard enough on his defense. And to make matters worse, he became obsessed with the idea that if he was on death row, he could get more attention and a better appeal.

It remains a mystery how Bobby got the phone privileges he did while in prison. It became a family joke. Here, Bobby was locked up, yet he was always the first to call Charlie's family with gossip of the town or news bits of the family. Eventually, the joke turned ugly. One Sunday night returning home from a trade show, they found a disturbing message on the answering machine. It had prison background noise and a man was screaming, crying, and threatening suicide if they didn't get him out of there.

During Bobby's next phone call, Charlie confronted him about his threat of suicide. He denied it being him vehemently. And due to the emotional trauma in the voice, they could never be sure it was him.

Nevertheless Charlie and his brother hired an attorney out of Nashville, Tennessee to help with

Bobby's appeal. They hoped this would calm him down emotionally, and he would drop his threats.

The lawyer read the transcript from the trial. He told Charlie and Barbara that in his opinion, Bobby had gotten a very good defense. The Nashville attorney went to the prison to see Bobby. He later told Charlie that Bobby had not given up on his vendetta of suing his lawyers. However, he told Bobby that he would not help him with that part of his appeal. He repeated that he felt Bobby had gotten a good defense.

The next conversation between Charlie and Bobby set fire to the phone wires.

Bobby made his cell as comfortable as possible.

The flames went higher when Bobby admitted that the Nashville attorney had told Charlie the truth.

He arrogantly informed Charlie that he and a fellow inmate with a law degree were going to work on that part of his appeal. And when he proceeded to tell Charlie how good "his jailhouse" lawyer was, Charlie lost it, and yelled, "If your jailbird lawyer is so damn good, what is he still doing in prison?"

Nothing Charlie said got through to his brother. To add insult to injury, Charlie's mom called every night hounding him to do something. Her pitiful cries tore at his heart as she repeatedly night after night picked his scabs by asking, "Don't you believe my boy is innocent of murder?" Night after night, Charlie would assure his mom that he believed his brother was innocent.

In time, her pitiful pleas took its toll. Worn down, Charlie became convinced in his mind that he had let her down. Maybe he should have done more to see that his brother had walked. He often repeated this to Barbara.

While this accusing enemy took a pot shot at his soul and mental peace, another enemy, more deadly, was eating away silently, destroying the hormonal and chemical balance of his physical body.

The physical and mental erosion was taking such a toll that he soon became a victim in his own mind. No longer able to view things clearly and reasonably, bitterness and hate soon became his best friends. He fumed in silence. His silent anger directed toward his mother and brother somewhat secretly salved his helplessness.

For four years, he had no escape from his nightly visitor. Sadly at age 80, his mother was found dead in the bed from a massive heart attack. Then his underground hostility began to spew, and his mind became a loose cannon. He lost all reasoning power whatsoever.

Daily, his rage spewed forth in one angry tirade after another. His dangerous fury scared Barbara

A family picture of the Howell children at their daddy's funeral. Bobby's dad died before there was any hint of Bobby being arrested. Left to Right, Front Row: : Lloyd, Walter, Helen, Charlie, Bobby. Back row: CJ, Bernice, Devon, Frances, Dovie, Herbert. The picture was taken at Charlie's house.

to the point of pushing him to see a doctor. One day, too tired to argue, he relented and went to see his family doctor. He was diagnosed with severe depression, a chemical imbalance, and emotional burn-out. At that moment, scared, he consented to the doctor's recommendation of treatment. Which was medicine and counseling. However, after three weeks of both, he gave his medicine a pitch and cursed his counselor, announcing he didn't have a problem. Barbara did!

He went back to work, slaving more hours than ever, totally living in denial, projecting his anger on his family. Eventually, Barbara persuaded him to get the free physical that was being offered at the plant where he worked. Blood in his urine landed him in the doctor's office once again. The doctor told him that he had an enlarged prostate gland and would probably need surgery at some point. But for now, there was no concern.

Charlie had no real symptoms, therefore he believed the diagnosis. He didn't even bother to get a second opinion or press for a biopsy that day.

He had come straight home from the doctor's office and went to work, totally oblivious to the tsunami that was headed straight for his body and his home.

A sign like the one that led to Cliffwood Estates in Lawrenceburg TN.

Quail Dr.

When the underground earthquake struck the Howell family, it was with a deadly force. Jeannea's husband was being stalked with murderous intentions by the spouse of a woman he was having an affair with at work.

The woman's husband had found a love letter and song, just one of many that Jeannea's husband had written to his wife.

Face to face, at his workplace, the man told Jeannea of how he had driven all over Lawrenceburg one Sunday trying to find them. The set of his jaw and the evil look in his eyes left no doubt in Jeannea's mind that this angry man had come for blood that Sunday. When unable to find Jeannea's family, he explained how he had returned home, believing that his wife had lied to him about where they lived.

He was wrong! His wife hadn't lied. His apparent knowledge of their small town told Jeannea this much. Yet, she didn't rise to the woman's defense.

"Do you live on Quail Drive, or is there a Quail Drive in Lawrenceburg?" his black eyes burned into hers, daring her to lie.

Jeannea didn't lie, accepting the sober truth that she might be included in this man's payback to her husband. She had summed him up quick. He wasn't just some man who had gotten loaded with booze and suddenly turned revengeful. No! This man had a mission. It became even clearer to her when he related without one ounce of repentance of how he had recently went to her husband's place of work—armed.

Frightened, she became instantly aware that with one wrong word she could become this man's enemy in a heartbeat. She saw a glint of steel respect strike his eyes when she refused to flinch as he purposely taunted by letting his black eyes rake her body.

Her back ramrod stiff, she refused to show emotion when he stated that he had every intention of blowing her husband away if he had walked out with his wife that day. Granted, she inwardly admitted she could feel a kinship, but not to the point of murder!

She told him she had no explanation as to why he couldn't find them that Sunday, which was true, until she went and found the road sign laying on the ground.

Cliffwood subdivision was nestled back out of sight of the main highway. There was only one turn off from Highway 64, the direction he had traveled that Sunday. Also, at this particular time the subdivision was still sparsely developed. With the sign down, it would have been nearly impossible for a stranger to have found them.

Jeannea knew in her heart her many tear-filled prayers had not changed the destiny of her husband, but she had no doubt, they spared her and her children from being involved in the blood-bath confrontation that this man had intended for the enemy of his home that Sunday.

She told him she had kicked her husband out, and had filed for divorce. She purposely left out that she had sued on the grounds of his admitted adultery and was forcing him to take an AIDS test with a follow up, and that both results were to be sent to her by registered mail.

Jeannea saw that his sore was salved somewhat upon learning that his enemy had been severely

Jeannea at work in the Murray Cafeteria. From left to right: Ellen Shedd, Jeannea Jones, Betty Clay, and Jewel Jackson.

punished. However, she was smarter than to risk her safety to this presumption. She packed up and moved in with her folks.

Daddy got her a job at the plant where he worked. If she worked a different shift than he, he would always go back to the plant and bring her home.

The threat of harm that hung like a shroud over his daughter and the inconvenience of having to be her guard dog took its toll upon Charlie. The undisputed truth of the meanness and abuse she had suffered, as well as his son-in-law's admitted adultery just piled up more emotional baggage for Charlie to lug around, which eventually hurled him over the edge. He became a ticking time-bomb.

True to her nature, Barbara grabbed the bull by the horns. She began a second round of child raising and was quickly cast into a new profession, a profession that she had fought so outrageously against with Charlie—woodworking.

Jeannea's job at the plant left her little time for building inventory for her craft shows. She desperately needed this extra income since she was getting no child support from her ex-husband. Soon, she and Barbara devised a plan. They would concentrate on making the children's stepstools, and let the sewing side of the business dwindle.

They assured Charlie that they wouldn't bother his work area. Frankly, they didn't want to share a workshop with him, so they set their equipment up on the far end of the basement from the former beauty shop. Both afraid of the power saw, they did ask if he would cut out their steps. He readily agreed.

True to his word, he soon had them well supplied with steps. Jeannea cut the sides of the little step stool out on her band saw before and after work at the bicycle plant. Barbara stained the many hundreds of pieces and placed them for assembly, which would prove to be their biggest challenge. Had they been knowledgeable, they would have built a jig to speed up the process. But now, determination was their biggest commodity—along with a hammer and nails.

They smashed fingers, bruised knuckles, and endured the pain of digging out enough splinters each night to have embarrassed a porcupine. Yet this torture didn't stop them.

Detroit City couldn't have shown any more pride watching their first car come off the line, than Jeannea and Barbara had upon seeing their first stepstool taking form.

Jeannea swung her hammer high and hard. She smiled big, watching her last nail sink fast and right on target. With a "go-to-hell smirk" on her face secretly aimed at her ex-husband, Jeannea grabbed the finished stool and quickly stood it in an upright position.

"Were we making a stepstool or a rocking chair?" Barbara asked sarcastically, glaring at the rocking stool.

"You don't think there would be a market out there for a rocking stepstool, Mom?" Jeannea grinned, as she rocked the stool back and forth.

"We're good, but I don't think we are that good," Barbara retorted. And then seriously asked, "What are we going to do?"

"Daddy might have an idea as to what we did wrong." Jeannea picked the stool up and hollered, "Daddy!"

"Yeah?" he poked his head around the shop door, then laughed when she showed him her rocking step stool.

"I can fix that on the power saw," he said, taking the stool.

They were excited and working hard. Their best show of the year was on the horizon. They felt they were ready despite Jeannea having been rolled to the graveyard shift at the factory, leaving her feeling horrible most of the time.

The beautiful October day dawned. They were set up at sunrise, excited, and ready to make money. This annual art and craft show attracted thousands, all ready to buy!

They sold 90 stepstools at $10 each. They were jubilant. However, in their busyness and excitement, they hadn't noticed their neighbor, who had enviously watched them all weekend.

In the late afternoon lull of the last day of the show, their neighbor ventured over for a friendly visit. They saw right off he was Mr. Macho Man. Yet, he acted helpful giving them some carpentry suggestions, and then to encourage the ladies, or so, they thought, he bought their last stepstool.

It never crossed their mind that Mr. Macho would go over their stool with a fine-tooth comb. But, he did. Not only that, he decided he could do a much better job than these wood-butchering ladies, who were out of their league.

He took their stool to the judges of the show and pointed out every little flaw and defect of the poorly made piece of carpentry. He told them this bad work was going to disgrace and ruin their craft show. The judges quickly agreed with Mr. Macho and threw them out of the show on the spot.

The next year at the craft show, Mr. Macho was there and showing off his carpentry. His shiny stool was built to perfection, and you could take it to the bank, no woman had driven a nail into it. This stool was all "Man Made." However, Mr. Macho didn't get rich with his beautifully made stool.

Jeannea's second job. These little stepstools were cut out on a band saw, stained, painted and assembled, and then personalized upon sale.

In fact, he was so disappointed with his sales, he didn't even bother to bring the stools back the next year.

Mr. Macho failed in his back-stabbing venture by making the same mistake that most bigots make. He didn't consider the whole picture. Of course, it was a given, the parents wanted a little step stool constructed safely. However, it is the beautiful artwork, and the free personalized names that made this product such a success.

They could truthfully say they had been initiated into the dog-eat-dog business world now. But, they didn't waste any time holding a grudge. Charlie was doing enough of this for everybody! They just worked harder and got more invitations to craft shows than they could possibly handle. They learned to pick the most profitable shows and gradually settled down into a routine, secretly thanking Mr. Macho.

Some of the shows Barbara and the gang launched into. For many years they worked 51 weekends per year at festivals, flea markets and tradeshows.

Charlie's many trophies from his coaching days of baseball and basketball. Also shown are trophies of his children and grandchildren.

Overworked, and stressed to a near breaking point with his brother's murder conviction, Charlie had become explosive and abusive, almost to the point of being a danger to his family. It had been four years since he had seen a doctor. Barbara pulled him out of bed every morning. She couldn't get past the fearful thought that there was something physical contributing to his emotional heartache.

His whole personality had changed. He had always had a gusto for life. Though small in stature, he sported an attitude that he was big enough to do anything he wanted to do! He was involved in church and he loved coaching ball, be it baseball or basketball. The many trophies that adorned his fireplace mantle not only spoke of his love but of his wins.

His gentleness and sportsmanship had now been replaced with bitterness and meanness.

Barbara was frightened and worried. His skin had a pallid gray look. His energy level was zero, pushed to action only by pure stubbornness. His eyes were dull and lifeless, often giving the appearance that no one was home in his body.

She fussed, threatened, and pleaded for him to see a doctor. Nothing moved him. She became a nervous wreck, hitting the walls of his excuses and denials on every turn.

Then one day opportunity knocked, rather unexpectedly. A good friend, whom they did craft shows with, called one afternoon. Barbara heard the phone just as she reached her laundry room. Giving the clothes basket a pitch, she raced across the basement and grabbed the phone on the third ring.

"Daddy went to the doctor today. He has prostate cancer." Barbara recognized Mary's voice immediately. Mary never chit chatted, but always got straight to her point. She possessed this kind of a personality.

"Is it operable?" Barbara asked, feeling punched in the stomach. She loved Mary's elderly father, and Mary was like a second daughter to her.

"Well, since Daddy is up in age, the doctor said something else would probably take him out instead of the cancer. He is going to do some kind of a treatment," Mary replied, totally without emotion.

"Well, I worry about Charlie," Barbara voiced her secret fears for the first time. "You know that doctor said four years ago he had an enlarged prostate gland."

"Daddy's doctor chewed him for not coming in quicker and getting that test."

"What test?" Barbara asked.

"It's called PSA. Daddy's doctor said all men should start the test in their forties." With this disclosure, Barbara perceived Mary had quizzed her Daddy's doctor.

Barbara probed further, hatching a plan.

"How do they give the test? And is it accurate?" In spite of her questions, Barbara remained tight-lipped.

"I reckon it's given through a blood test. I don't know about the accuracy, but Daddy's doctor sure did push it." Mary then ended her conversation as abruptly as she had started it.

Barbara cradled the phone and walked back across the basement. Her mind was busily digesting her friend's information as she dumped the dirty clothes in the washer. Closing the door to the laundry room, she didn't head back up the stairs as usual. Instead, she walked briskly toward the woodshop, her jaw set.

She opened the door and poked her head inside. Charlie looked up but didn't say anything, still pouting from an earlier fight.

"Charlie, I just talked to Mary, and she said her Daddy went to the doctor today, and he has prostate cancer."

The silence became deafening.

"How bad is it?" Charlie asked, finally.

"Evidently, not too bad. At least, that was Mary's impression from what I gathered. The doctor told her dad that due to his age something else would more than likely take him out," she paused, and then added, "but, the doctor also said something about a test. PSA. I think that is what she called it. You know it has been four years since you went to the doctor." She hesitated, aware, she was treading on dangerous ground.

"I got no time for a doctor," he snapped, the glint in his eyes warning her not to push. He waved her away and went back to his wood sorting.

"Well, you will have time to die," she flung back over her shoulder, aware her words were drowned out by the noise of the power saw.

She couldn't get her friend's news off her mind. Finally, she risked the lion's den by taking matters into her own hands. She called their doctor and made an appointment for Charlie to get this PSA test. And before she lost her courage, she raced down the stairs and yelled, "Charlie!"

"Charlie!" she yelled louder, standing in the doorway of the woodshop. At a glance, the determined look on her face told him he wasn't going to ignore her and get by with it. Not this time. He reached over and cut the power saw off and stared at her with pure hatred in his eyes.

"I called the doctor and made you an appointment for that test."

"What test?" he asked in pretense.

"The one, that Mary was talking about," she didn't wait for his reply, but high-tailed it back up the stairs, hearing him swear like a sailor.

He would keep the appointment! She knew him. He would keep the appointment.

As the doctor's appointment got closer, Barbara fretted, and Charlie worked harder. He continually harped about having to lose time going to the doctor. Barbara stayed mum, aware he was trying to pick a fight so he could walk off in a huff, and spite her by not going to the doctor.

Within 24 hours after seeing the doctor and having his test, the doctor's nurse called and asked to speak to Charlie. Barbara handed him the phone and walked out of the room.

Later, he came into the kitchen where she sat, looking shell-shocked.

"What did they say?" she asked, bracing herself for what she expected to hear.

"My PSA test came back very high."

"How high?" her voice trembled.

"24."

"What is normal?" she whispered.

"Zero. Or 0.1," he answered, showing a humbleness she hadn't seen in a long time.

"What are they going to do?" she asked, masking her fear.

"The doctor wants to repeat the test."

"When?" she asked, seeing he wasn't the least bit suspicious.

"Two weeks."

"Why wait two weeks?" she stormed, unable to hide her shock.

"To see how aggressive it is, I reckon."

This answer made no sense to her. Everything she had ever heard about this disease was get to it as fast as you can. Then the thought struck—he didn't know what was going on because he hadn't asked.

Finally, he broke the silence by asking, "That's the only reason they could have to wait, ain't it?"

His question quickly confirmed her thoughts. He hadn't asked the doctor one question.

She didn't fuss at him. She was learning in her old age. She hadn't changed him in 34 years. She wasn't going to change him now. But she did unload her opinion. "Well, I'd venture to say you have had this cancer for four years. This was the problem when they found blood in your urine when you took that physical at the plant. Yeah, I know this PSA test is new but that dumb doctor should have done a biopsy four years ago." She got angrier and louder as she spoke. Not just at the careless doctor back then, but at Charlie also, for not taking full responsibility for his own health.

The next two weeks were hell for both! Barbara compensated by worrying. Charlie walked around like a zombie and refused to discuss it.

The test was repeated. And both secretly imagined the worst.

And it came! His PSA had jumped up to 26 in just two weeks. The doctor made him an appointment with a cancer surgeon in Nashville, Tennessee immediately.

The surgeon didn't pull any punches. He talked straight to Charlie and Barbara. He explained, that Charlie had a very aggressive type of prostate cancer. And he said it would kill him if he didn't have radical surgery. Charlie was in shock. He was only 54. The doctor admitted in regard to Barbara's question, that yes, it was usually true that this cancer didn't strike until the late 60s and 70s. Even then, usually not with this type of aggression. He stressed again that Charlie's life was at risk.

In regard to this, the only option he gave Charlie was radical surgery. He stated further, that he had no way of knowing if it had invaded until he got in there, and if the worst was there, Charlie would have to take chemotherapy.

Luckily, the cancer was still confined to the gland. The doctor used extreme caution while doing the surgery, putting Charlie's life first thought. For this, they were very thankful, but the mop-up was a bitter pill to swallow. Charlie lost his bladder control and his sexuality. A tough blow for a man of 54.

Of course, they traveled in the "If Only" tunnel for weeks. This cancer is so curable and usually without terrible mop-ups when caught in the early stages. The hits that Charlie had taken in his personal life since his brother's conviction, and the continual saga of dealing with his mother night after night, no doubt had had a contributing factor in Charlie's health issues.

But, why didn't he shake it off as others had, and resume his private life?

Why? Barbara has asked this question a million times or more.

Why couldn't Charlie turn the page and get on with his life despite his brother's conviction of six life sentences? The answer was four square. He was totally wiped-out—mentally, emotionally, physically, and financially.

He was so overcome by delusion and confusion that he made it difficult for anyone to help him. To be more precise, at this point in time, he was totally unreachable. He felt he bore the shame alone and licked his wounds the only way he knew how. His every waking moment was spent in anger, maliciousness, and spite.

Sadly, now, he lived only to hurt. And he got good at it! He shredded his immediate family's emotions and physical well-being beyond repair, enforcing the age-old truth that hurting people hurt people.

How did this gentle, God-fearing, good husband, father, and grandfather become so overtaken by bitterness and anger that he became totally void of human emotion? It took 10 years, two psychiatrists, two psychologists, and Charlie spending a week in a Nashville mental hospital to answer this question for Barbara. She came to realize that Charlie had been brain-washed.

Brain-washed? By whom? His mother. Charlie's mother had programmed him from the cradle to believe that his older brother, Bobby, was special and untouchable.

When Barbara and Charlie were first married, Barbara saw quickly that her new mother-in-law's attitude was such. No one was to bring her son, Bobby, to task. No one. Not wife. Not daddy. Not God! And certainly not the law. For mama enjoyed, and often bragged to Charlie and Barbara about some of her "special" son's daring and lawless capers.

While high on medication, as she often was, his mom would hint that brother Bobby had done Charlie a big financial favor in his youth. They got the impression that this so-called favor wasn't exactly within the law. But when they pushed for information, she would suddenly clam up.

They would have never taken anything she said seriously, except for the memory of an incident that had happened to Charlie one night coming home from work. Charlie's car caught on fire under the hood, and after putting the fire out, he walked to Bobby's house and asked him to take him home.

The next morning when Charlie went back to see about his car, he found it burned. Charlie called his insurance agent without suspicion at the time. They sent an investigator out and Charlie told him what had happened. The insurance agent investigated and gave no impression that he suspected arson. At this time neither did Charlie, other than he was of the opinion that the fire had been totally put out the night he walked away from the car.

One day in a high mood, his mom made a subtle hint about what a man could do to a stalled car. From that moment on, especially after Bobby's fires escalated, Charlie and Barbara often wondered if Bobby had reset the fire on Charlie's car.

There was ample opportunity! The conked-out car was left less than a mile below Bobby's house and having carried Charlie home that night, Bobby had to pass the stalled car to get back to his place. Aware it was useless to confront Bobby, they filed their suspicions and got on with living.

Then, years later, something Bobby did turned their thoughts back to their burned car.

Charlie became suspicious that Bobby might have set him up with the intentions of using him for an alibi.

It happened in this fashion: A few days before one of Bobby's house fires, Charlie had called and asked Bobby to go to Franklin, Tennessee with him to look at a car that Charlie and Barbara were thinking of buying for a young boy who went to church with them. Charlie had left home early that particular morning to pick up Bobby.

His brother came out of his house pronto and got in the car with Charlie.

Charlie was backing out of the driveway when suddenly Bobby asked him to stop, saying, he had to go back into the house. Charlie didn't think a thing about it until they got back home and found that Bobby's house had burned to the ground. Charlie could never shake the picture from his mind of Bobby going back inside his house. At this time already having had several houses to burn, only Bobby's mama, and perhaps his immediate family, believed Bobby's tales of bad luck.

Did Bobby do something inside his house while Charlie waited in the driveway? Charlie didn't know. But he would always believe it was possible, and if that's so, he believed that his brother had intended to use him for an alibi.

Suspecting this, neither Charlie nor Barbara were comfortable with Bobby's alibi at his trial. Their doubts were strongly enforced when one day in particular they were at his mom's house visiting his sister, the sister who was Bobby's alibi at his trial.

No fishing in mind, Charlie said somewhere in their conversation, "I sure hope it's true that Bobby had nothing to do with that nursing home fire."

"I sure hope so, too," his sister added in agreement.

"What do you mean, you hope so too? You should know! You said you were with him all the time the night of the fire," Charlie exploded, rising to his feet, his face red with anger.

His sister quickly amended what she said, and tried to convince Charlie and Barbara that it was just a slip of the tongue. But from that day to this, Charlie nor Barbara believes the alibi.

Still, it would be many years, more for Charlie than Barbara, before the whole truth would settle down inside their hearts.

Why so long? It took years for their insight to walk away from the courtroom drama that happened during his brother's trial and go to the jury room where justice and truth prevailed.

The biggest stumbling block for Charlie was the witness's testimony of the *how*.

"They lied," he harped. "The state's witnesses lied and our defense attorney proved they lied."

From what a member of the jury told Barbara later in regards to how the jury had arrived at their verdict, Charlie was right. The jury believed they lied.

Yet, they convicted the man? Yes. How? Why? The prosecution proved their opening statement at the trial. Which was? *Bobby Howell burned this business to take over this business.*

The prosecution proved this statement, in spite of their lying witnesses, and the laughter in the courtroom when the defense attorney had mocked them about their "outrageous statement."

Yes, they proved to the jury beyond doubt, then to Barbara, and later to Charlie, that Bobby Howell burned the business to take it over and six people lost their lives in this terrible act.

Barbara and Charlie's wilderness walk in regard to his brother's guilt to this crime was the motive, or to be more specific, the lack of a motive. Yes, they believed it possible that Bobby had been guilty of arson many times.

If they believed he was an arsonist, then what was the struggle with the motive of this terrible crime?

The pattern. His gain. They couldn't see either!

In fact, this was their whole defense of him when they hired their lawyer. They never painted Bobby Howell lily white, but, they just couldn't see the ear marks of Bobby's pattern on this horrible crime.

You see, Bobby didn't own the nursing home, and therefore no insurance money was forthcoming. Better stated, there was no gain for him.

But, stranger than fiction, the prosecution proved motive and gain, without hiding the fact that the property belonged to his ex-wife, and he was married to another woman.

Maybe he burned the business to spite his ex-wife? This motive was discussed heavily during jury deliberation, Barbara was told. But the Howell family knew this couldn't possibly be true. His relationship with his ex-wife has never been one of this nature.

The tide finally began to turn for Charlie after getting knowledge and understanding of the pyromania-compulsive personality.

Some days, he still rocked back and forth in his quest for the whole truth. His inability to pinpoint his brother's pattern in this crime always brought him pangs of doubt. He couldn't totally justify in his mind the harsh conviction without stronger evidence of the pattern. Charlie is a simple man, and it just didn't make sense that a man would burn a business to take over the business.

Yet, Charlie had no qualms whatsoever about believing that his brother had the pyromania-compulsive personality.

One day, spurred on by Barbara to examine their inside information, he readily agreed that their first-hand knowledge of his brother's emotional state the morning of the fire did indeed cast a lot of doubt toward his brother's innocence. But when they got down to the brass tacks and probed in depth their own actions the morning of the fire, they both reeled with shock. Until this moment, other than a gut feeling and the slip of the tongue of his sister, they had no concrete proof that his brother's alibi was a fabrication. Each read the other's stunned expression when the evasive truth struck.

You see, upon hearing about the fire that morning, Charlie and Barbara had rushed to the scene, thinking Bobby and his daughter could have been involved. A friend had called Barbara after hearing it on the local news at seven o'clock. Barbara and Charlie had arrived at the scene no later than 7:20. Their neighbor, who worked at Murray Ohio Manufacturing, Inc. with Charlie, and was also a fireman, was still at the scene. Tommy told Charlie what little he knew about the fire and the victims. Minutes later they left and went straight to his mom's house. They pulled up at the same time Bobby and his new wife did.

Both noted, and talked later about how nervous Bobby had been that morning. Without speaking to either of them, Bobby had stepped out of his car trying to light a cigarette. He was pale and drawn. Both of his hands shook so badly he couldn't light his cigarette. When they related to him that they had been to the fire, he never asked the first question. Charlie and Barbara both became suspicious of his fright. They even went so far in their thoughts, that one or the other, asked the question later, "Could it be that Bobby was afraid of being framed with this crime?"

They all stayed and jawed awhile with his sister and step-dad, Mr. Collins. Their hindsight told them clearly that the alibi tale told on the witness stand didn't happen. It was the timeframe, this was the give-away. Charlie and Barbara were with *both* at mama's house at the time they had said otherwise. Also, in their recollection, due to the transmission on sister's car being blown the night before, Bobby and his new wife had come to take his sister to the hospital for the first time to see mama since her arrival from Florida.

It was heartbreaking for Barbara to watch Charlie's frantic search for truth. Was he going to make it to the finish line? She often doubted it.

Some truths he learned made him feel as if he were jumping in bed with the enemy. Truths, he had first overlooked, totally ignored, or thought to be insignificant began to stick in his mind like glue.

Truths that he could prove with factual knowledge would often sink him into depression and resentment for weeks.

For one, the testimony of the owners of the nursing home. This brought him the most anguish. They proved at the trial that Bobby had gone to the courthouse and legally tried to have them evicted from the nursing home, that he didn't own legally. That day in court, believing that the owners held a grudge due to the fact they had lost a son in the fire, this important piece of evidence slid right past Barbara and Charlie.

Years later, a re-reading of the transcript of the trial caused Charlie to remember a certain phone call he had gotten from Bobby. He had told Charlie that he and his daughter were watching the nursing home while the owners had taken a trip to Texas. This explained why Charlie and Barbara had rushed to the scene upon hearing about the fire.

This wasn't so!

True, they found out at the trial he had been asked to help oversee the home. Not with his daughter, but with a young resident by the name of Terry Walker who lived there. Charlie and Barbara learned at the trial, also, that while the owners were gone, Bobby had eloped with Terry moving her and another resident to his house. Not only that, he was in the process of trying to have the former owners evicted from the property due to a lapse in insurance. Of course, he failed to mention any of this to Charlie when he called him that night. He knew that Barbara and Charlie were under the impression that he and his ex-wife were back together.

He bragged to Charlie that night what a perfect financial set-up this place was, and even went so far as to tell Charlie right down to the penny of what the place was bringing in when they counted the senior citizen's checks.

Why would Bobby call Charlie and tell him all this? Because Charlie was always hounding Bobby to get a job. Bobby had lost a good job when he walked out during a wildcat strike years ago at the same place where Charlie was still employed. At the time of the strike, the brothers lived next door to each other. One brother walked the picket line and the other brother crossed the picket line every day to work.

This was a very trying time, especially hard on family relationships. At a little country store where both brothers traded, Charlie was often told about the bounced checks his brother had written to them. Embarrassed, Charlie always covered the bad checks.

Bobby had never really kept a steady job since the strike.

A year prior to his brother's arrest, Charlie would often call his brother about a certain job. He was never interested due to the wage.

This was hard for Charlie to understand, because his brother had no job and no wage. His new wife unemployed, Charlie and Barbara were always curious of how Bobby managed to live. They had often speculated to each other that he might be into the drug scene.

However, the very first week after Bobby was arrested their curiosity about his finances was put to bed.

Stressed to the max, Charlie came home one evening from his mom's house just fuming.

"I've found Bobby's employer," he announced sarcastically. "No wonder I could never get the boy a job."

"I'll bite—who?" Barbara teased, suspecting what he was going to say.

"I had to take over mom's bills and banking today. She was giving Bobby money, right and left," he said, his resentment showing.

"Giving? Or was he stealing?" Barbara asked, very serious now.

"Take your pick. Either could be right," he snapped, leaning back in his chair, only seconds later to add, "I know she bought a piece of land from him for $5,000, and he knew she couldn't get a clear title."

"Why couldn't she get a clear title?" Barbara plopped down in the nearest chair.

"It's all tied up in his arson insurance crap," Charlie answered, fingering his remote control and swearing angrily when he didn't get a picture.

"And you think, she didn't know about this before she bought the land from him?" Barbara's attitude reeked of pure mockery.

"Well, she led me to believe that he didn't tell her. But who knows. They're two peas in a pod." He pitched his remote towards the couch. "The thing that's the hardest for me to understand in this whole mess is why would anybody be so stupid as to risk jail time by burning something that belonged to an ex-wife."

"He didn't. You and I both know that property was his. If the real truth was known, probably his and mama's."

"Well, the title was in his ex-wife's name," Charlie said, showing no animosity.

"True. But it didn't become hers until he married that ole gal," Barbara sneered in glee. "Bobby got trapped by the system. He played it one time too many. You know as well as I do, Bobby was always buying things and putting them in other folks' names. When the Parkers found out this property was in his ex-wife's name only, and made a new lease with her, it surprised your brother."

"I'll give you that," Charlie snorted, and then turned serious by adding, "This pyromania compulsive personality knowledge that I'm learning, the doctor says there are usually certain triggers that causes this personality to act." He stopped speaking, aware Barbara was lost in his explanation. "What I mean to say, there is some sort of pressure that is usually pushing them."

Barbara nodded, and asked point blank, "Do you believe that Bobby had this pyromania compulsive personality?"

"Yes. It's a given. You know me and my brother counted 14 fires he had before his trial."

"You and who?" she asked.

"Me and Calvin," he answered. "Yeah, I believe he had the pyromania compulsive personality, more so now, than ever, since I've remembered a conversation that me and Walter once had."

"What did your brother Walter tell you? Have I heard this?" she asked in puzzlement.

"Probably not. To be honest, since I couldn't remember the incident, I took it with a grain of salt," he was speaking honestly now and without his usual pent-up anger.

His next words confirmed further to her that he wasn't harboring any resentment. He spoke very calmly saying, "I believe now what Walter told me."

"What did Walter tell you?" she nudged him, unable to curb her curiosity any longer.

"He said Bobby set his bed on fire when he was a child."

Her mind flashed back to his explanation of the pyromania compulsive personality. She said slowly, without a hint of mockery, "You do know the trigger."

"Huh?" he was slow catching her drift. "I know the trigger?" he asked, looking at her in disbelief.

"Yeah, you have just said it. Think. Who did you just now say was Bobby's employer?"

"Mom," he answered, slowly.

"No. Not entirely now. Remember? It was brought out at his trial of how he had gotten possession of Terry's check—but a high price tag came with that!"

She glanced at him and saw he didn't have a clue as to what she meant by her remark!

"What I mean Charlie, Terry wasn't the sweet, little ole girl, he thought she was. Remember how mom told you, she had gotten mad one night, pulled a knife on Bobby and went so far as to threaten to call the police, and tell them he had burned the nursing home? In all actuality, that girl may have known something to have threatened your brother like that!"

"To be truthful, that thought has often crossed my mind," he said. "You know Bobby would get frantic when he thought the prosecution was going to question her?"

"In all honesty Charlie, dealing with your obsessions has given me some insight into this whole trial," she said. "You know the state proved in court beyond a reasonable doubt that property belonged to your brother. When the Parkers drew up a new lease with Bobby's ex-wife, his money-making plans were gone. All he had left was a young pregnant wife. I think the property matter became an overriding obsession." She looked at him to gauge his reaction.

He didn't appear offended by her bluntness.

She pushed further by asking, "How many times did you and him carry mom to the emergency room before you wound up at Columbia hospital?"

His pain visible, he said, "This was our third trip to the emergency room in just a matter of a few weeks. I'll admit, he and I both thought that mom was going to die." He paused, but only for a second, and then added, "That's the reason we decided to take her to Columbia that night. They weren't getting to her problem at our local hospital. You know the second time they hospitalized her here at Lawrenceburg they told us she had TB. Scared everybody to death! They made us all mask up when we went out to visit."

The angry pout on his lips that she knew so well hinted that he was receding back into the past. She feared him flipping over into an angry mode. She stayed mum. The silence became deafening.

Finally, when he showed no sign of moving on, she prodded by asking, "Isn't it true that they told you and Bobby at the hospital that night in Columbia that she might not make it?"

"That's right. They said she had viral pneumonia."

His facial expression quickly changed. She knew his thoughts had made a turn from anger to reason, and that was progress. "Bobby took it hard, didn't he?" she asked.

He nodded, looking down.

"Believing he had been taken hostage by his ex-wife and the Parkers, Bobby's emotions were already fried. Bang! Suddenly, he finds himself in another hostage situation. His mom—the one person he could depend on was maybe dying, and there wasn't one thing he could do about it." Barbara watched him closely and fearfully.

"I don't doubt any of what you say. In fact, I'm totally convinced," he stared off into space.

"Do you remember the letter he wrote to us from prison right after mom died?"

He nodded. Then said, "I think Bobby loved mom as much as he was capable of loving anyone."

It wrenched her heart to watch his painful struggle. Yet, she knew it was necessary. He had to come to some degree of acceptance of his brother's accountability, if he was to ever regain control of his own life and emotions. At this moment, she felt he was getting there. However, his next statement quickly raised a red flag.

"I'm glad that jury member told you that they hadn't believed he intended for anyone to get hurt. I think that was partly the reason for him being so upset that morning we saw him. It didn't go as he had planned, and those people got killed." He looked at her for encouragement.

"You do understand that your brother had to be punished, don't you?" Barbara asked, watching him closely.

He nodded, but she wasn't totally convinced.

"You know this was a personality disorder, just like your passive aggressive behavior. But, neither of these personality disorders, yours or his, erases your accountability, right?" she asked, fearful that he would perceive some false conclusions, if she didn't keep it in his face. It was her belief, that Bobby Howell had received mercy from a jury that was divinely picked.

The jury had laid aside in their deliberation the distorted version of the *how* as told by the witnesses. This was told to Barbara by a jury member and led Barbara to believe that nothing but Solomon's wisdom could have led this jury to see so many concealed truths with such accuracy.

Hard truths. Truths that were totally illogical and outrageous to the simple, natural mind. But she, as the jury, and now Charlie, believed it happen! The man burned the business to take over the business. No, he wasn't intending for anyone to die. The jury believed this. Barbara and Charlie believed this. But, it happened.

Bobby died in prison, after having served only seven years.

Jeff and his sister, Jeannea. The only reason this picture was taken, was because Jeff's mama was bigger than him. She could make him stand there, but she couldn't make him like it.

her battered prodigal

The fruit doesn't fall far from the tree. Strong willed, Barbara's son didn't readily bow to circumstances he didn't like, even as a child. Having to make his bed every morning before school was a hard pill for him to swallow.

"This is sissy work," he often argued. He and mom had many hellish fights about this 'sissy work.'

One morning, fed up with his harping, she set about firmly correcting her son's mind on this girl-work after catching him trying to outsmart her on his bed-making.

"Why are you sleeping on top of this bedspread?" Barbara gave the sheet a yank, exposing her seven-year-old, warmly nestled in his Superman pajamas.

"He said it was 'sissy work' and stupid for him to have to make up his bed every morning before school. Why, he just hops up and smoothes off the wrinkles, and his bed is made," the informant was his 6-year-old sister who stood in the doorway, her eyes sparkling with hero-like worship.

"So, it's girl-work and stupid to have to make up your bed every morning, right?" Barbara glared at her first-born.

"Yeah," he didn't crawfish, knowing he was asking for a lecture and punishment.

This boy thought so much like her, she could usually tell what he was going to do before he did it, but that wasn't to say, he wasn't a worthy opponent. He was.

She had to manage his type-A personality with caution. He had a genius IQ and was a whiz at math. His teachers would often call him, and even tell their students to call him, when they couldn't work a math problem. This did nothing to help Mama curb his ego. He surfed right through high school and college with excellent grades, rarely cracking a book at home. Despite dropping out of college for a year to intern with Union Carbide, he had still graduated with his classmates with high grades.

Barbara worried frantically when she sent him off to college. He steered clear of all drinking and partying while in college. Parental love. Church training. Knowledge. These weapons had so exposed the enemy that peer pressure held no threat for him.

It helped that mom had been totally honest and shoved no family secrets under the rug. He knew that his Granddaddy Davis, his mom's dad, had died in the gutter at the age of 52, a wasted life.

He wouldn't have said he believed in generational curses or that sins of the father were passed down to the sons, but he wasn't dense enough to push his mom's theory.

Upon graduating from Tennessee Tech in 1984 with an electrical engineering degree, he went to work the first week after graduation. Alone in the deep south, he settled comfortably into his Monaco Lake apartment just inside the city limits of Pascagoula, Mississippi. He soon adapted to bachelor living.

One Sunday morning, a few months later, the relocated Tennessean rushed into the Baptist church, late. He sneaked into the pew glancing around, hoping no one had noticed. He wasn't that lucky. Across the aisle, the pretty blonde smiled at him with a knowing look.

He gave her a lop-sided grin and wondered how this girl had escaped his notice.

He couldn't have told you one song the choir sang that morning or one point that the preacher made in his sermon. Stealing glances at this seemingly uninterested girl across the aisle, his mind was devising a plan. Not one to let grass grow under his feet, he soon knew enough about her to fill an encyclopedia. When learning she had a steady boyfriend, her appeal was suddenly enhanced. He was quickly spurred into action.

If Barbara's first-born could have been accused of having a vice it would have been his gusto for competition. He had been known to get so caught up in competition he often let it push him over the edge of not showing respect for boundaries. This case in point, it didn't faze him that she was taken.

Barbara worried about this character trait, fully aware it hinted of rebellion and selfishness. She often pondered if it could be the first cousin to the demon of destruction that followed her family tree.

Full of himself, this recent college graduate showed the girl's high school suitor no mercy.

Jeff and his beloved little Midget. He was a senior in High School.

The chase ended soon with the displaced Tennessean capturing the prize. The wedding date was set—she would be a beautiful June bride.

Sadly, just hours before the elaborate wedding march, the Howell family got a sneak preview of their son's trophy. Mom wept, aware her son was being hijacked by young love and ego, and was as blinded as America would be on 9-11.

His future wife got offended at a member of the wedding party, as well as her mother-in-law to be. The outrageous temper tantrum and venom this little blonde girl spat, sent Barbara reeling. "Stop this wedding!" Her mind screamed in fear.

"Too late! Too late!" her reasoning shot back.

She couldn't have felt anymore helpless than if she been riding a run-away train with no conductor at the throttle. She was scared of hanging on, but more terrified of jumping.

The fighter that she was, why didn't Barbara force the enemy's hand? Because at this time, her enemy had no face.

Would years later have made a difference in her stand that day? You bet. Ten years down the road, this enemy would have been quickly unmasked by her personal experience and education by the National Alliance on Mental Illness. Instead, that day she sat passive, trapped in a maze of warnings. Her thoughts raped by the scenes taking place before her eyes.

The preacher smiled as the young couple turned, and he introduced Mr. and Mrs. Jeff Howell to the wedding guests. It was uncanny how much Barbara identified with the father spoken of in the Bible when he had given his son his ticket to the far country.

Barbara quickly scrubbed her fearful thoughts with reason. All this girl needed was love and acceptance. Barbara's compassionate nature was battling her horse sense and winning that day, for she truly believed real love would change her. Right? Wrong.

Father Time would teach Barbara, as well as her son, that this belief was an illusion. This beautiful young girl had an uncontrollable anger problem. Deep-seeded anger. Fueled by pride and a victim's mentality.

This was the early 80s and people's knowledge of the seriousness of domestic violence was still on the run-way. At this time there were no anger management classes, nor support groups. It would take the loss of many lives of spouses, co-workers, and children before this problem gained national attention for outside involvement and really got the help it needed.

Just a few weeks into the marriage, the Howell family began to suspect the worst. In their ignorance, they just hoped it would go away. It didn't! This young girl's emotional problems spilled over and left radioactive fall-out that took years, and a new love, to bring about a total recovery in their son.

What pushed her button to give Jeff a peek into her split personality?

A super job offer. A manufacturing company located in South Carolina, very selective in hiring, had instructed a head-hunter to lure Jeff over for an interview.

Upon hearing this, Jeff could hardly wait to share his good news with his new wife. He didn't foresee any problem. For his career plans had been nailed down before his marriage, or so he thought. Being honest and forthright, he had told her it was just a matter of time before he left the deep south and his present job.

His reasons? Several. Union problems for one. Unsafe working conditions with no plans of improving the facility was another. (They shut the plant down within 10 years of him leaving.) Health problems. Some were serious enough he couldn't ignore. Due to his exposure to chlorine, he had already develop eye irritations which had forced him to discard his contacts. His exposure to this chemical was unavoidable as it was used in most areas where he spent a large portion of his day as a project and electrical engineer.

However, his eye problems were minor in regard to his throat problems. He suffered constantly with sore throats and laryngitis, which he had been told could have some long-term side effects.

In a previous discussion of a job move, his soon to be wife, assured him there would be no problems to her leaving Mississippi with him. Despite her young age, 18 at the time, Jeff had no reason to doubt her. Especially when she related of how she had been moved around all her life by her daddy's career, and gloated by saying, "I have survived that in one piece, haven't I?"

One can't begin to imagine his shock when he rushed home to tell her the good news. Right before his eyes, she became a wild woman! Going into a rage, she yelled about how daddy moved her around all her life and how much she hated it. Then she preceded to tell him about the horror

Jeff, a freshman at Tennessee Tech in Cookeville, Tennessee.

Jeff, now graduated and working at International Paper in Moss Point, Mississippi.

of always being the new girl in school, always being left out, and never really being totally accepted.

When raged out, she said stubbornly, "I'm not moving. Not this time! Daddy has finally settled down and built a new house. And I'm not budging! I'm not about to give him the satisfaction of seeing me start moving around now."

When Jeff got over his initial shock, understanding smacked him over the head. His wife was full of deep-seeded anger. Hurtful, vindictive anger! Aimed straight at daddy. She was blinded to the fact that her anger spilled over into all her relationships, which is true for most of this terrible enemies' victims.

In their obsessed mind, all they understand is that someone owes them something. In their twisted confusion, they demand that someone, usually someone other than their original offender, pick up the tab.

"What kind of she-devil have I married," Jeff muttered. "Doesn't the woman understand she could become a young widow?"

She didn't care! This truth socked him right between the eyes. Her vindictiveness killed any capability she had to love. This instant insight and understanding into her personality sent a deep chill to his heart.

He rushed to the kitchen. He had to get out of her presence.

Moments later, his back ramrod straight he came back to where she was and said, "I'm going for that interview. If the job is what I've been told, and if it is offered to me, I'm taking it. You can go or you can stay! And quite frankly, I don't give a damn which you choose. You lied to me!" He whirled and walked out the front door without a backward glance.

"Stupid! Stupid!" He beat himself up and castrated his ego. "I'll never trust another woman!" He vowed, pounding his steering wheel in fury. "She lied! She lied," he screamed. Seconds later, feeling the cast away, he became powerless to stop the loud bitter echo ringing constantly in his ears. *She lied! She lied!*

Jeff got the job. She moved and made his life hell.

He put her through college, built her a new house with white carpet, and hired her a maid. And he went to the Ramada Inn, with or without her, due to her moods, to visit his parents when they came to town to see him. She made it plain to Jeff that she didn't want visitors messing up her castle.

Jeff never admitted to anyone he made a mistake in marriage. But eventually even the mighty fall!

It took seven years, but he finally crashed with a loud bang. To be more precise, he crashed with an expensive bang!

An expensive bang that he, as well as mom and dad, would pay for, for years to come.

Barbara was home alone when his news came. She got the phone on the second ring, the ID telling her it was her first-born.

"Hello," she settled comfortably in her recliner with intentions of having a long chat with her son.

"Mom, what are you doing?" She picked up his war fatigue immediately.

"What's wrong this time?" she asked, ignoring the trap of small talk.

"I've called her daddy to come and get her," he said, his guard down.

Pain stabbed her heart. Her boy had never failed at anything. A marriage failure was not something that you wanted to cut your teeth on. She feared repercussions.

Her fears materialized. Hurting people hurt people. Her son's emotions had been in deep freeze for seven years. Now, wife gone and he alone, his protective shell began to crack. As layer after layer was being peeled, each painful exposure carried a high price tag, and not just to him, but to all who loved him.

His seven years of silent anger was the most devastating. When his feelings began thawing he began to spew. He spewed anger at mama. He spewed anger at God.

He mocked and abandoned the Christian values he once held so nobly.

Unchained, he renewed an old love—one he had met while in high school. Tennis.

This once cast-away love was soon number one in his life. He was by no means a pro in tennis, but he was good. The many trophies decorating his fireplace mantle proved that. He had trophies for singles wins. He had trophies for doubles wins. Tragically, his teammates were not only good tennis players, but they played the wild side of life with recklessness as well.

To Barbara's horror, she learned her boy was traveling with this wild crowd at a break-neck speed, fast becoming a rich playboy! This escaped prisoner was now enjoying his new status with gusto! He let his mama know real quick that he didn't have any intentions of being rescued.

Her boy didn't have a clue to the depth of mama's love for him. She put her fighting britches on, grabbed her Bible, and enlisted prayer partners all over the country.

Her answer came! She had to get her boy back to Tennessee, shower him with unconditional yet tough love that would protect, while his bottled emotions were being uncapped.

Barbara was smart enough to know this divine answer was only her focus point. She knew her next step would require Joshua's courage and Solomon's wisdom as this question pounded her mind: How was she going to get her prodigal back to Tennessee?

Her prodigal hadn't come to himself. He wasn't in the literal pig pen feeding and eating with the pigs as the prodigal spoken of in the Bible.

Just the opposite! Her son had achieved all his goals in the far country. He was Mr. Success with the intelligence of knowing he had arrived!

You could take it to the bank, Mr. Success was way over-qualified for any job in her area. He was top-notch educated, holding an electrical engineer degree from Tennessee Tech University in Cookeville, Tennessee, as well as a master's degree in business from the University of South Carolina. He had computer knowledge and countless hours of experience in solving automation problems and control.

March 27, 1994

234-Help Wanted

WANTED
Experienced paper cutter operators, folder operators, multi-color offset press operators, estimators, and printing salespeople for a locally owned printing company. Send resume to Dale Johnson, P.O. Box 1514, Decatur, AL 35602 or call 205-353-8991. Benefits include vacations, holidays and insurance programs.

WANTED—OTR drivers. We're looking for a few good drivers for a 10 state southeast area. Home most weekends. Flats, vans. Minimum 23 years old, 1 year recent verifiable OTR experience. Even if you aren't planning to change jobs, call Buddy, Billy Barnes Enterprises, Monville, ALA. 1-800-844-6458

S & LABORERS above average ly 7-4, WORKS

439-Business Opportunities

AUTOMOTIVE
PRECISION TUNE
FRANCHISE AVAILABLE
803-345-3624

☞**BUSINESS FOR SALE**☜
North Alabama manufacturing company. Automotive related. Well established with solid customer base. Good cash flow to owner. Strong asset base. Good small to midsize firm. Owner financing available.

Free list of North Alabama businesses to potential business investors

CLEANING AND RESTORATION Business $36,000 including inventory, training, and ongoing support. Call 1-800-826-9586.

DISTRIBUTE HERSHEY New

The newspaper clipping advertising businesses for sale.

Employed for the last seven years by the most successful tire manufacturing company in the United States, he, as well as, his co-workers were looking forward to spending two years in France at some point in their career level.

Barbara didn't come close to having the net or the lure to entice her son back to his small hometown. Still, mama didn't waver.

One day while leafing through the classified section of her home town newspaper, she noticed an advertisement. Soon her heart began to race. She had found the *how*.

The advertisement told of businesses for sale. One was a well-established business located just 39 miles from her small town. Hurriedly, she picked up the phone and called her son.

To her great surprise, he put up no argument but asked her to send him the paper.

She had expected a cat and dog fight. Why had he caved in so quickly without the least bit of struggle? Time would tell!

Screws and more screws. This was Jeff's ticket out of the far country. And eventually cast him on a road to love and happiness, he didn't dream possible.

Summer was at a perfect stand-still. Barbara stared out the big picture window, taking no notice. Her tormented mind was asking questions and getting few answers.

Questions of why?

How?

How could a business end its first year with 1.2 million dollars in sales? Then in spite of serious set-backs, recover, making good profits into the third year before suddenly starting to tailspin?

She sorted her thoughts, unable to escape one nagging thought. Lack of communication.

As certain scenes played out before her eyes, she became even more convinced that all the key players in this business operation were at fault, her son included.

Her son flat refused to let her in on any of his business decisions and would only tell her things when they were past fixing. This aggravated her to no end. She had sunk a lot of money into this venture with him. Watching him make mistakes that could have been avoided had he consulted her sometimes caused her to lose sight of the real issue at hand, *getting her prodigal out of the far country.*

In her brooding, she ignored the ringing intrusion. But when the telephone refused to hush, she moved to view the ID, seeing the intruder was her son.

She sent the hurried prayer upward, "Please, God! Let no crisis shadow my pathway today."

Did she have a premonition?

She would have answered no as she picked up the phone and said, "Hello."

"Mom, my bank account has been frozen!" His words went right over her head, but she immediately picked up the panic in his voice.

"What do you mean?" she asked.

"I mean the IRS has frozen my bank account. And this means I can't make my payroll this week." She immediately plugged her one good ear with her finger to blot out his angry, cussing tirade.

"Why would they do that?" she asked, when he stopped to catch his breath, bracing herself for another angry response. And it came!

"Cause I have had no damn money to pay their taxes. You know the hits that I've been taking. Some of my customers aren't paying, and hardly any pay on time. In fact, some time ago, I turned a delinquent customer over to a bill collector, who has been owing me $12,000 for over nine months. And I just learned this morning, the bill was collected and the collector has skipped town with my money."

"Did your customer prove to you that they paid the bill collector?" she asked.

"Absolutely," he snorted.

"Can't you swear out a warrant for the collection agency or something?"

"Yeah, if I had the money and knew where they were," he sneered, going off on another angry tirade.

"Well, you can't escape death or taxes, son," she sighed, in a somewhat defeated manner.

"Right!" he snapped, his offense smacking her in the face, jerking her back into reality.

"I'm sorry, son," she immediately apologized, aware that a lecture was the last thing he needed this morning.

"You need a lawyer," she said. "A good one! If the stories are half-way true of what I've heard about the IRS."

"Well, I'd like to know how I'm to hire a lawyer. Remember? My bank account has been frozen. I have the IRS after me. I can't make payroll, and right now, I don't have money to buy a good pot to pee in. Of course, if you know a good lawyer that works for free, I'll take him." He went for the juggler, unaware she wasn't listening. She was hurriedly raking back through her morning paper.

"Get a pencil, and write this number down, and call him and see if he will help you. And remember, there's always Monday after Friday." She was in full support of her battered prodigal but she was not blinded to his mistakes, mistakes he had made by the numbers.

Some mistakes he made in ignorance. Some mistakes he made in arrogance. Some mistakes he made in direct rebellion and spite toward her and women in general.

But for the most part, the mistake blaring in their faces right now was one of blind trust and youthful mismanagement. To put it bluntly, he had been taken in by a selfish, greedy seller and some eager-beaver broker, dying to make a sale.

His granddaddy mistake was defying King Solomon's advice and living with a contentious woman for seven years. But that was in the past now. Barbara refused the ticket to travel down that road. Instead, her mind raked the coals of memory in their beginning and failure of this venture at hand.

A few days after she had mailed her son the advertisement, he called to tell her that he had already set up an appointment to talk to the broker about this particular business.

Spite and vindictiveness his advisors, he shared little with her about this business venture. When she had pressed for information, she remembered he seemed to be pleased upon his first meeting of the seller. But to his financial disaster, he learned too late that this guy wasn't the "good ole Alabama red-neck" he portrayed.

Mistake number 1: Jeff put too much trust in his fellow man. Despite his business sense, he over-looked the seller's hesitancy when he first asked to see the books. He accepted their refusal when they said something to the effect, "We have to be more certain of our deal first."

Not a total moron, he asked point blank if they had one customer who made up 40 percent or more of their business sales.

To this day, he can not tell you how they satisfied his mind on this question without lying, other than he must have been taken in by something they had implied.

Mistake number 2: When Jeff had taken over the books and saw his suspicions were true, he should have immediately addressed the problem. However, the customer's smooth transition of his new ownership had enabled his dallying and fooled him into assuming they were there to stay. In his take-over, they never varied in the least in their buying power.

Mistake number 3: In just a short time of ownership, Jeff realized he should have hired a lawyer to sort this sale out for him. A good lawyer would have questioned certain things he let slip, like their asset sheet.

He hadn't been owner long before he realized he had been grossly overcharged for some old tooling and other things that were completely unusable.

The first year alone he spent $60,000 on tooling.

As the employees began to warm up to him, they got loose-lipped. Soon he heard a disturbing rumor, one he desperately hoped wasn't true.

But it was.

Six months into his ownership, his "best customer, (40 percent of his sales)" assuming Jeff had been told, called one day to let him know they were almost ready to move into their new facility.

Jeff cussed himself up one side and down another. Having been forewarned, he should have stuck to his guns and questioned more about this big customer.

But even now, totally aware of some things in this whole charade that went far beyond just being a shrewd business man on the owner's part, Jeff still didn't want to believe bad about his new friend. However, he couldn't ignore the pulsating question that tormented his mind day and night, *Did the former owner have prior knowledge that this customer was leaving?*

Some of Jeff's employees were certain that he did.

He was told by more than one employee that the seller not only knew this customer was leaving, but he had tried to sell them his factory.

Was this true?

Jeff hoped not and quickly turned his attention to surviving and counting his assets. His most outstanding asset was, in his opinion, his excellent manager. A manager who was grossly overpaid, despite his love for hard work and great people skills. Still, Jeff was glad to have him onboard and secretly thanked the former owner for having him.

A few months before Jeff bought the factory, the former owner had hired a friend to come and manage the factory for him during a short-term illness. A veteran in the screw business, this man knew all the ins and outs of screw manufacturing.

In fact, he had proven himself so capable that when the former owner returned from the sick bed to take back over his business, he suddenly didn't want to sell.

This, Jeff knew was factual. For when the broker called and told Jeff the seller no longer wanted to sell, Jeff pressed the broker for information.

The broker said, the seller related to him that his manager was making him so much money he'd be a fool to sell.

Jeff was disappointed and felt somewhat cheated at this news but took it in stride.

Then a few weeks later, the broker called back and told Jeff his seller was ready to sell again.

Mistake number 4: Jeff should have never thrown his hat back into this ring.

Mistake number 5: Jeff compounded mistake number 4 by not being suspicious enough to question "why" the sudden change of the seller's mind now to sell, when just weeks prior, he had been so adamant in not wanting to sell.

Mistake number 6: Jeff banked his curiosity and focused on the information he had learned from the broker. He contacted the manager personally and offered him a job at a hefty salary. The out-of-state man agreed, and they shook hands to seal the agreement.

Eventually, the cost of that handshake would come to haunt Jeff for years to come. A simple handshake? Yes. Why? Because it invisibly welded two men together as partners, trapping each one in deceit and greed for their own personal reasons.

Unbeknownst to the manager, Jeff contracted the former owner to stay on the work force for six months to help in his transition. Thrown together, day in and day out, the former owner and his former manager weren't very happy. Jeff sensed right off that something was not quite right between the two men.

Was it dislike? No. Jeff wouldn't say that. If anything, it was more of the nature that they shared a guilty secret.

Mistake number 7: He should have paid more attention to his gut feeling and less to his engineering logic.

However, he got so busy making money, he ignored his suspicions and they soon faded into the background of his mind.

Sales, his very first month, were over $100,000. Barbara took $50,000 to their bank and paid off their remaining down payment. Jeff fully intended to have this business paid for within three years.

He worked hard and soon recovered from the one big customer's leaving who had taken almost 40 percent of his sales. He simply replaced them with several small customers, which was nothing but good business sense.

His victory was sweet but short-lived. Another rumor surfaced.

This nasty rumor cast a lot of doubt to the credibility of both the former owner and his manager, and confirmed Jeff's suspicions of a shared secret.

Jeff rolled in his bed at night now, fully aware he could be plucked like a chicken. Not once, did he ever doubt but what the rumor was true. It filled in too many blanks. For one, it explained fully, the reason of the seller's change of mind to put his business back on the chopping block, when only days before, he had been so adamant not to sell.

The big question that constantly raked Jeff's mind was, when had the former owner learned the his good friend and manager was soon to become his competitor in the screw business?

Jeff knew it hadn't been an up front issue, for in his short term of business dealings with the manager, he knew better than this. No, he figured the former owner had trusted his friend completely. Then later hearing his manager was to become his competitor, the former owner had panicked and put his business back up for sell.

Jeff couldn't respect the former owner's business tactics, but he could certainly identify with his fear. This manager had kept mum when Jeff had hired him and now he had untold knowledge of Jeff's business.

And not only that, Jeff figured he had made several donations to his manager's new business operation. For some days now, Jeff had suspicion his new tooling had been disappearing.

At first, Jeff assumed his thief to be his prize employee. He set a trap hoping to be wrong, because this employee could run a machine like no one else. He had on several occasions run a million screws in one day. The only catch, the boy wouldn't show up for work more than two or three days a week. Jeff suspected dope.

Jeff's trap failed to catch his thief.

But two days later, a call from the local jail cleared his suspect of thievery. However, his suspicions of dope were confirmed. The young boy had been arrested and was jailed on possession. While his young employee was incarcerated, Jeff had more tooling disappear. He didn't have to hire Ben Matlock to find his thief. He was positive who it was now.

Eventually, Jeff was able to bail the young guy out of jail and talked him into getting help by promising him he would hold his job.

Tragically, the young boy crashed his motorcycle and splattered his body all over the Tennessee River bridge before they got him into rehab.

One month before his year was up, Jeff's plant manager informed him he was leaving.

"Why?" Jeff asked, pretending surprise.

The manager refused to meet his eyes, mumbling, "My factory is ready for production. I was in the process of building when I came here to help my friend who was sick."

"Spare me your phony bull," Jeff silently screamed, somehow mustering up the courage to hide his smirk.

Mistake number 10: Jeff accepted the fact that he'd committed a businessman's suicide. He neglected to draw up a protective contract with the manager. Not only that, but he extended his southern hospitality and trust futher by letting the out-of-state man bed down in his office to save on motel bills.

In all probability this unscrupulous man not only had a list of all the old customers of the former owner, but all of the new customers he had busted his tail to get as well.

Still, Jeff wouldn't accept defeat. He just took on another hat. Now he was owner, manager, and set-up man. He learned how to set-up every machine, pushed to the edge by these guys taking advantage of him when they didn't want to do a hard job. Their idea of job security was, you don't show anyone anything. They were clearly unteachable, when it came to learning teamwork. It was totally foreign to them.

Jeff survived by sheer willpower.

Jeff and his beautiful bride, whom he has been married to over ten years.

He crossed over into making screws for the car companies and began mass producing rivets.

His business was almost paid for and he was ready to strike it rich. He had eventually been able to take some good steps toward his employees by setting up an insurance plan and paid vacations.

Then comes China's manufacturing boom.

Where Jeff had been working 14 hours a day, now he began to work 16 hours a day.

This enemy was not just taking a bite out of him. It was trying to gobble him up and spit him out.

He was in over his head before he awakened to the fact he couldn't compete with this giant. He found he was spending high dollars on tooling only to bail these car companies out of a bind while they were waiting on their China boat.

Once the China boat arrived, he never heard from them again for future business and some not even to pay their bills.

He was dog tired. He was angry. He was fighting a losing battle. And finally, he faced it.

This was where he was the morning he called mom with his bad news about his bank account.

But once he asked for help, he got it. Barbara backed him to hire lawyers and business consultants. They helped him walk out of his business problems honorably. The best advice he got was to take the big step, and buy his own building and quit paying the ridiculously high rent to the former owner. At the new place, he eventually phased out the failing screw business and launched into another market, a market that has become a huge success. He manufactures a cabinet that is placed in a large hardware store chain, scattered throughout the United States. This cabinet houses their knife display. He works directly with their knife manufacturer.

He also makes a line of smaller display cases and has several distributors for these. His dream of owning his own business has been achieved despite his many setbacks.

He has been married over ten years to a beautiful Alabama girl, who works right by his side along with their two dogs, Sassy and Jasmine.

Above: One of Jeff's display cases made for a large hardware store.

Right: A sliding drawer display case, made by Jeff.

Business&Finance

C-1

Southern Ladies mean business

5 Tips

On Effective Leadership

1. Communicate clearly and routinely. Lay out your company goals and principles in a mission statement and keep sharing your vision with your employees.

2. Involve employees in setting objectives. Give them feedback on how they are progressing toward meeting those targets.

3. Give your people authority, then hold them accountable. But don't go after them personally when things go wrong. Find out first if the process is at fault.

4. Be accountable yourself. Install an advisory board or executive team to help you make good strategic decisions and give you feedback on your own performance.

5. Be trustworthy and extend trust to your employees. That will help you earn their loyalty and strengthen your company.

On How to Protect Yourself from Employee Lawsuits

1. Obey the laws regarding employees. Don't discriminate in hiring, for example, or permit sexual harassment.

2. Hire carefully. Look for people with a strong work ethic and avoid hiring those who feel life owes them something.

3. Adopt strong employment policies. Communicate them clearly to employees and enforce them.

4. Keep good records on employee mistakes, even when they're not firing offenses. Document your own actions and the reasons behind your employment decisions.

5. Consider buying employment-practices liability insurance (EPLI).

On Resolving Disputes

1. Consider adopting an alternative dispute resolution (ADR) program as a way to resolve employer-employee conflicts. It can be less costly and time-consuming than litigation.

2. Understand that ADR uses such tools as mediation and arbitration and is conducted in private.

3. To find help in setting up an ADR program, look in the Yellow Pages under "Mediation Services." Ask other small business owners or your local chamber of commerce for referrals.

4. Remember that ADR programs work best when you have a clearly written ADR policy that employees see as fair. Start by maintaining an open-door policy that encourages employees to bring grievances to their managers with-

---

By DAISY MOSER
Front Page Correspondent

Most Americans put in their years at the company, waiting anxiously for the day they can retire, sit back, relax and take life a little easier.

One 64-year-old Oklahoma woman doesn't have retirement slated on her agenda anytime soon.

Barbara Howell of Broken Arrow in recent weeks has moved the headquarters for her thriving business, Southern Ladies' Showcases, from Tennessee to the Tulsa area.

"I ain't going to retire," Howell said. "I'm going to burn out, not rust out."

Southern Ladies' Showcases originated 12 years ago when Howell sold a softer line of products, crocheted toy clowns for children.

"We sold $50 worth at our first craft show and thought we had a landslide," Howell said.

From its humble beginning the business grew. Products began to change from clowns' to children's furniture to the now-popular wooden-framed, glass-front showcases. As demand began to grow, so did the production staff to include Howell's daughter and two granddaughters.

And so did time on the road.

The adventures on the road aren't confined to merely traveling, Howell said. The sale of the product yields great tales and the business has received some unusual custom orders.

"One man, an archeologist, wanted a custom-made showcase to display his collection of artifacts," said Jerrica Jones, Howell's granddaughter, the business's hardware specialist and driver and a freshman biomedical chemistry student at Oral Roberts University.

"He wanted to display his collection of human skulls. He measured his wife's head there at the show in order to see how big the case needed to be."

Southern Ladies Showcases have also sold 164 cases for a regular patron in Illinois to display his collection of 9,700 fishing lures. An Alabama customer has purchased 50 cases to display his 15-year collection of McDonald Happy Meal toys. Yet another gentleman from Tennessee has purchased 19 cases to house his 454 model trucks.

A 12-year-old Nashville boy collects Pez dispensers and has bought enough of the Ladies' showcases to house his 250-piece collection. One customer ordered a garment case to display an Aerosmith jacket that was signed by each group member. One gentleman bought a case to display a chunk of the Berlin Wall.

Finally, one steady customer is a former husband of Patsy Cline, Charlie Dick.

With a tight schedule of back-to-back craft fairs in a variety of locations, the family has had to hustle to reach their destinations on time. As a result of this harried agenda, the family has racked up 19 speeding tickets between the drivers.

"I've had five, but talked my way out of all but two," Howell said. "One time a cop pulled me over with my loaded trailer and said, 'Where you going?' I told him to the flea market. He said, 'Oh is that this weekend? Okay, then. Just cover your load up, and get on out of here.'"

There have been some traveling mishaps as well. One accident involved both Howell vehicles, traveling caravan style.

"I yielded and she didn't," said Jeannea Jones, Howell's daughter, family business bookkeeper and ORU Office Coordinator of Building and Grounds. "Well, at least we kept it in the family."

The show had to go on.

With one vehicle totaled and the other undrivable, the products still had to arrive on time. The family had the trailer packed with inventory towed to the next show so sales could continue.

"And then there was that time we almost hit the Shiners" collecting money at a stoplight, Jeannea Jones said, giggling.

Although a veteran in the craft, Howell has run into a few obstacles in her production schedule. Whenever she hits a snag, she has a sure-fired method of problem solving.

"Jesus was a master carpenter," Howell said. "I'll say, 'You know all about carpentry. Help me with this.'

"He'll either show me or send someone to show us how to do it."

Jennifer Jones, granddaughter, ORU senior video graphics design major and part of the Ladies' production team, trained and managed three teenage boys from her own high school that worked in production after school and on weekends.

"The boys were older than me, but I knew a lot more about the business than them," Jennifer Jones said. "I worked fine with them at the house, but they wouldn't speak to me at school. "I was their boss at home but beneath them at school."

Jerrica Jones has found her niche in the enterprise. Her greatest strength is her ability to pilot a two-ton truck pulling a 24-foot cargo trailer into tight spaces. A petite blonde who hit the road at 16, Jerrica Jones has discovered she has an innate ability to park the massive vehicle in areas most veteran drivers have difficulty navigating.

The craft industry is a vibrant and growing network of small businesses, according to the Craft Organization Directors

---

INFO BOX:

Southern Ladies' Product Line
Showcases
- Garment case
- Arrowhead case
- Knife case
- Model cars cases, all sizes
- Thimble case
- Golf ball case
- Baseball case
- Football case
- Basketball case
- Shot glasses case
- Derby glasses case
- Coin case
- Marble case
- Memorial flag case
- Shadow box

Children's furniture (hand painted & personalized)
Stepstool
- Toy box
- Table & chair set
- Rocking chair
- Baby doll cradle
- Pegged coat rack
- Desk

Hand painted saws
- Landscapes/wildlife saw blades
- Landscape/wildlife antique handsaws

Southern Ladies' Showcases
Broken Arrow, OK
918.519.4445
According to the Craft Organization Directors Association Web site www.craftassoc.com, the Craft Industry Economic Impact Survey Results indicate that the industry's demographic profile shows.
- 64 percent of craftspeople are female.
- 41 percent are between the ages of 46 and 55; the median age is 49.
- 79 percent of craftspeople work in a studio located on or their residential property.
- 78 percent are members of a craft organization.
- 64 percent work alone in a studio, 18 percent work with a partner or family member and 16 percent work with paid employees.

The family has mols

Fast forward to August 12, 2002. A pit bull named George Jones, along with two women and two teenagers left the security of their small Tennessee town to take up residence in the big city of Tulsa, Oklahoma.

They left little behind in personal belongings. Their 27-foot fifth wheel, that was to become their home, was crammed full of clothes, quilts, sheets, and cooking utensils. Their 24-foot trailer was over-loaded with power saws, sanders, drill presses, nail guns, compressors, wood, glass, and several general items that carpenters use in their woodworking.

Jeannea had no prospects for a job. Barbara had no workshop. JJ was enrolled in Gateway Christian School in Memphis, Tennessee and wasn't the least bit excited about being home-schooled the next four years. Jennifer had gotten a 30 on her ACT and had taken the $25,000 scholarship that was offered her at Oral Roberts University, aware this university was ranked very high in the nation among colleges for its music and graphic design majors.

Their savings for this transition were gone, totally wiped out in their rebounding from the actions of someone beyond their control. These ladies had to regroup and prioritize in order to focus on food and shelter while regaining momentum for plan B to find funding for Jen's college. Their only commodity at the moment was their Joshua courage and Solomon wisdom.

Upon their arrival in Tulsa, they set their "home on wheels" up in the Warrior Campground, located a few miles from the university across the Arkansas River.

When the weekends rolled around, they hitched up their trailer and fifth wheel and headed out for Texas, Arkansas, Missouri, and other close-by states that advertised flea markets or gun shows.

The owner of the campground was always there to see them off, and not only that, he also knocked off two night's pay from their weekly rent. For this, they were grateful, but this man went the extra mile. Every Sunday night, upon their late arrival back to the campground, they never had the hassle of trying to find a vacancy. No sir! Their spot was always ready and awaiting their arrival. And this was the way it went the six months they lived at the campground.

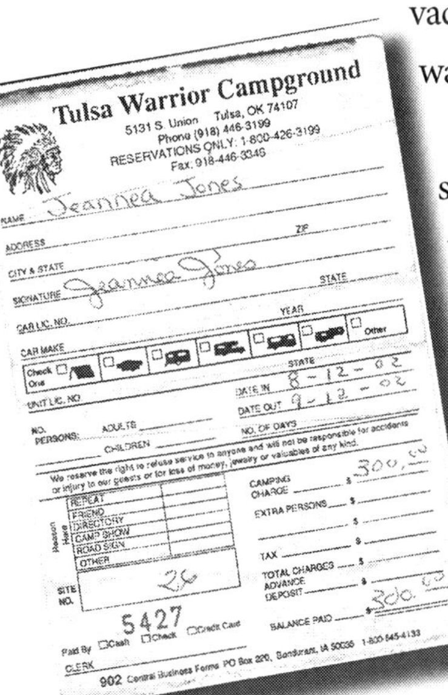

Their biggest hurdle in this Oklahoma town was finding a work shop. It was six weeks before Barbara found an affordable workshop. How did she cope until then? She worked at her weekly shows carrying her equipment with her in the 24-foot trailer. Even to this day, she has never found good, affordable supplies in Oklahoma. For the most part, she hauls wood and glass back from Tennessee to work the winter months in Broken Arrow, Oklahoma, and spends her summers working in Tennessee.

Their first winter in Tulsa was a grizzly. As the summer paled into fall, and fall faded into winter, coming from the South and used to mild winters, they began to ask around to find out what to expect of the winters in Oklahoma.

They were told that usually the winters in Oklahoma were mild. By the first of December, they became very aware that an Oklahoman and a Tennessean were poles apart on their understanding of *mild* winters.

Their fifth wheel was getting more uncomfortable by the day. Their water was frozen every morning, and their gas bills were getting higher than their monthly rent. They slept cold despite mounds of cover, and Jeannea traipsing out at 2 a.m. every other night to change out the propane gas.

The last week in December, they moved into an apartment, and shortly thereafter, two eight-inch snows blasted Tulsa, sending them scurrying for snow tires and teaching them how to cope with *mild* winters in the wild West.

But eventually, things began to look up, Jeannea got a job at the university. However, this cut her traveling out, and Jen's schooling got harder and more demanding, and this pulled her off the road, as well.

Barbara and JJ began to pull the long hauls. As soon as JJ turned 16, she got her driver's license and eventually took over most of the driving. However, their longest haul occurred just a few months before JJ turned 16.

Coming in from a 10-day show from up North, Barbara was in the driver's seat for a whopping 19 and a half hours. She did break-up the trip somewhat by pulling off at a Wal-Mart parking lot in Conway, Arkansas to get a few winks.

In 2005, Jeannea bought a beautiful home in Broken Arrow, Oklahoma. It sported a big back yard for George Jones, and a workshop for the business. Soon the news got out about a bunch of southern women running a wood shop. Tulsa Front Page newspaper sent their correspondent Daisy Moser over to get an interview.

Tulsa Front Page

Business&Finance

Southern Ladies mean business

WEDNESDAY
September 28, 2005

By DAISY MOSER
Front Page Correspondent

Most Americans put in their years at the company, waiting anxiously for the day they can retire, sit back, relax and take life a little easier.

One 64-year-old Oklahoma woman doesn't have retirement slated on her agenda anytime soon.

Barbara Howell of Broken Arrow in recent weeks has moved the headquarters for her thriving business, Southern Ladies Showcases, from Tennessee to the Tulsa area.

"I ain't going to retire," Howell said. "I'm going to burn out, not rust out."

Southern Ladies' Showcases originated 12 years ago when Howell sold a softer line of products, crocheted toy clowns for children.

"We sold $50 worth at our first craft show and thought we had a landslide," Howell said.

From its humble beginning the business grew. Products began to change from clowns to children's furniture to the now-popular showcases.

With a tight schedule of back-to-back craft fairs in a variety of locations, the family has had to hustle to reach their destinations on time. As a result of this harried agenda, the family has racked up 19 speeding tickets between the drivers.

"I've had five, but talked my way out of all but two," Howell said. "One time a cop pulled me over with my loaded trailer and said, 'Where you going?' I told him to the flea market. He said, 'Oh, is that this weekend? Okay, then. Just cover your load up, and get on out of here.'"

There have been some traveling mishaps as well. One accident involved both Howell vehicles, traveling caravan style.

"I yielded and she didn't," said Jeannea Jones, Howell's daughter, family business bookkeeper, and ORU Office Coordinator of Building and Grounds. "Well, at least we kept it in the family."

The show had to go on. With one vehicle totaled and the other undrivable, the products still had to arrive on time. The family had the trailer packed with inventory towed to the next show.

"He'd either show me or send someone to show us how to do it."

Jennifer Jones, granddaughter, ORU senior video graphics design major and part of the Ladies' production team, trained and managed three teenage boys from her own high school that worked in production after school and on weekends.

"The boys were older than me, but I knew a lot more about the business than them," Jennifer Jones said. "I worked fine with them at the house, but they wouldn't speak to me at school. I was their boss at home but beneath them at school."

Jerrica Jones has found her niche in the enterprise. Her greatest strength is her ability to pilot a two-ton truck pulling a 24-foot cargo trailer into tight spaces. A petite blonde who hit the road at 16, Jerrica Jones has discovered she has an innate ability to park the massive vehicle in areas most veteran drivers have difficulty navigating.

The craft industry is a vibrant and growing network of small businesses, according to the Craft Organization Directors Association Web site www.craftassoc.com. The industry's first major craft economic impact survey released in

Hand painted saws
• Landscape/wildlife saw blades
• Landscape/wildlife antique handsaws

Southern Ladies' Showcases
Broken Arrow, OK
918.519.4445
According to the Craft Organi-

• Maul chest case
• Pistol chest case
• Ball glasses case
• Derby glasses case
• Coin case
• Marble case
• Memorial flag case
• Shadow box

• percent of craftspeople are female.
• 41 percent are between the ages of 46 and 55; the median age is 48.
• 79 percent of craftspeople work in a studio located on or in their residential property.
• 78 percent are members of a craft organization.
• 64 percent work alone in a studio, 18 percent work with a partner or family member and 18 percent work with paid employees.

per year.

With the business going full steam ahead, Howell is a long way from retirement. She has an

Jennifer Jones said.

Jeannea Jones feels her mother's energy is "off the charts."

"She runs circles around me,

The family has made many sacrifices in order to keep the business thriving. The Jones girls grew up on the road help-

Southern Ladies Mean Business

By Daisy Moser
Front Page Correspondent

Most Americans put in their years at the company, waiting anxiously for the day they can retire, sit back, relax and take life a little easier.

One 64-year old Oklahoma woman doesn't have retirement slated on her agenda anytime soon.

Barbara Howell of Broken Arrow in recent weeks has moved the headquarters for her thriving business, SOUTHERN LADIES' SHOWCASES from Tennessee to the Tulsa area.

"I ain't going to retire," Howell said, "I'm going to burn out, not rust out."

Southern Ladies' Showcases originated 12 years ago when Howell sold a softer line of products, crocheted toy clowns for children.

"We sold $50 worth at our first craft show and thought we had a landslide," Howell said.

From its humble beginning the business grew. Products began to change from clown's to children's furniture to the now-popular wooden-framed, glass-front showcases As demand began to grow, so did the production staff to include Howell's daughter and two granddaughters.

And so did time on the road.

The adventures on the road aren't confined to merely traveling, Howell said. The sale of the product yields great tales and the business has received some unusual custom orders.

One man, an a archeologist, wanted a custom-made showcase to display his collection of artifacts," said Jerrica Jones, Howell's granddaughter, the business's hardware specialist and driver and a freshman biomedical chemistry student at Oral Roberts University.

"He wanted to display his collection of human skulls. He measured his wife's head there at the show in order to see how big the case needed to be."

Southern Ladies Showcases have also sold 164 cases for a regular patron in Illinois to display his collection of 9,700 fishing lures. An Alabama customer has purchased 50 cases to display his 15 -year collection McDonald Happy Meal toys. Yet another gentleman from Tennessee has purchased 19 cases to house his 454 model trucks.

A 12 -year-old Nashville boy collects Pez dispensers and has bought enough of the Ladies showcases to house his 250-piece collection. One customer ordered a garment case to display his Aerosmith jacket that was signed by each group member. One gentleman bought a case to display a chunk of the Berlin Wall.

Finally, one steady customer is a former husband of Patsy Cline, Charlie Dick.

As demand for the showcases has increased, so have the miles on the road required to distribute the product. The family has had up to three vehicles on the road and puts 50,000 miles per year on them. The family is in production five days per week producing 300 units weekly and then travels 51 weekends per year to sell, every weekend but Christmas.

With a tight schedule of back-to-back craft fairs in a variety of locations, the family has had to hustle to reach their destinations on time. As a result of this harried agenda, the family has racked up 19 speeding tickets between the drivers.

"I've had five, but talked my way out of all but two," Howell said,. "One time a cop pulled me over with my loaded trailer and said, "where you going?' I told him to the flea market. He said, "Oh is that this weekend? Okay, then. Just cover your load up, and get on out of here."

There have been some traveling mishaps as well. One accident involved both Howell vehicles, traveling caravan style.

"I yielded and she didn't," said Jeannea Jones, Howell's daughter, family business book-keeper and ORU Office Coordinator of Building and Grounds. "Well, at least we kept it in the family."

The show had to go on!

With one vehicle totaled and the other un-drivable, the products still had to arrive on time. The family had the trailer packed with inventory towed to the next show so sales could continue.

"And then there was that time we almost hit the Shiners" collecting money at a stop-light," Jeannea Jones said, giggling.

Although a veteran in the craft, Howell has run into a few obstacles in her production schedule. Whenever she hit's a snag, she has a sure-fired method of problem solving.

"Jesus was a master carpenter," Howell said. "I'll say, "You know all about carpentry. Help me with this."

"He'll either show me or send someone to show us how to do it."

Jennifer Jones, granddaughter, ORU senior video graphics design major and part of the Ladies' production team, trained and managed three teenage boys from her own high school that worked in production after school and on weekends.

"The boys were older than me, but I knew a lot more about the business than them," Jennifer Jones said. "I worked fine with them at the house, but they wouldn't speak to me at school. I was their boss at home but beneath them at school."

Jerrica Jones has found her niche in the enterprise. Her greatest strength is her ability to pilot a two-ton truck pulling a 24-foot cargo trailer into tight spaces. A petite blonde who hit the road at 15, Jerrica Jones has discovered she has an innate ability to park the massive vehicle in areas most veteran drivers have difficulty navigating.

The craft industry is a vibrant and growing network of small businesses, according to the Craft Organization Directors Association Web site www.craftassoc.com. The industry's first major craft economic impact survey released in April 2001 revealed as many as 126,000 crafts people are working in the United States today. Their average gross revenue per person is $76,025.

The total impact of craft sales is $12.3 billion to $13.8 billion per year.

With the business going full steam ahead, Howell is a long way from retirement. She has an exorbitant amount of energy to burn and a never-ending passion for the business.

"It's divine, because there is no way she should be able to do what she does at 64 when we can't keep up with her at 21," Jennifer Jones said.

Jeannea Jones feels her mother's energy is "off the charts."

"She runs circles around me," and I'm 17 years old," Jerrica Jones said. "She gets up early and starts to work, I wake up to the sound of the saws running in the basement. And then she's still working after I quit at night."

The family has made many sacrifices in order to keep the business thriving. The Jones girls grew up on the road helping at the fairs. The four women have traded in the luxury of relaxing holidays and sporting manicured nails for nights and weekends operating high-powered table saws, radial arms saws, five-foot drill presses, band saws, glass cutters and air guns too craft their stock.

This is not a path I would have chosen," Jeannea Jones said, "But I know that the time the girls have spent with mother and the business has put a maturity in them that a lot of kids their ages do not have. It developed their relationship with people and ability to deal with the public

"It's uncomfortable. But it has taught us a level of independence we didn't already have. We're better women for it."

An antique saw that once belonged to another transplanted southerner,
David Roach, who gave it to Barbara when settling his dad's estate.

armed, and dangerous

Thirteen years ago, in debt to her eyeballs, Barbara Howell took over a business that her sick husband had abandoned.

She learned to run power saws and drill presses with the same gusto that she had pumped a hairdresser's chair and cut hair. She hit the road to market her goods, fully aware, she was way out of her league. She would have been much more comfortable driving a Ford tractor as she once had when farming her 200-acre farm and delivering her feeder pigs.

Barbara wasn't on the road long before she became armed and dangerous. She became armed with experience and know-how as she mined a man's world of making money. Many times, she did it in fear and trembling, refusing anything less than prosperity.

She became dangerous to the credit lenders. Slowly, but surely, she paid off all her debts, the pledge she had made to her church's building fund, and the line of credit debt she had taken out for her son to purchase his business.

More than that, she operates her business on a cash-only basis. All her rigs are debt free, including the 27-foot fifth wheel, the four-wheel-drive, three-quarter ton GMC truck, a dual cab, three-quarter-ton Chevrolet, her 24-foot cargo trailer, a 10-foot cargo trailer, two 16-foot flat bed trailers, and eight acres of prime land in which she has future plans for building a new factory.

Despite all her pain, sweat, and tears, Barbara wouldn't trade one mile of where she's walked these last 13 years for any amount of money.

She treasures her many friends, some, whom, you will be meeting in the following pages. She adamantly feels richly blessed by her acquaintance of all her customers, who are scattered all across the United States and Alaska.

success!
all over the map

Just some of the many states and cities, in which our showcases are housing special keepsakes for our many customers.

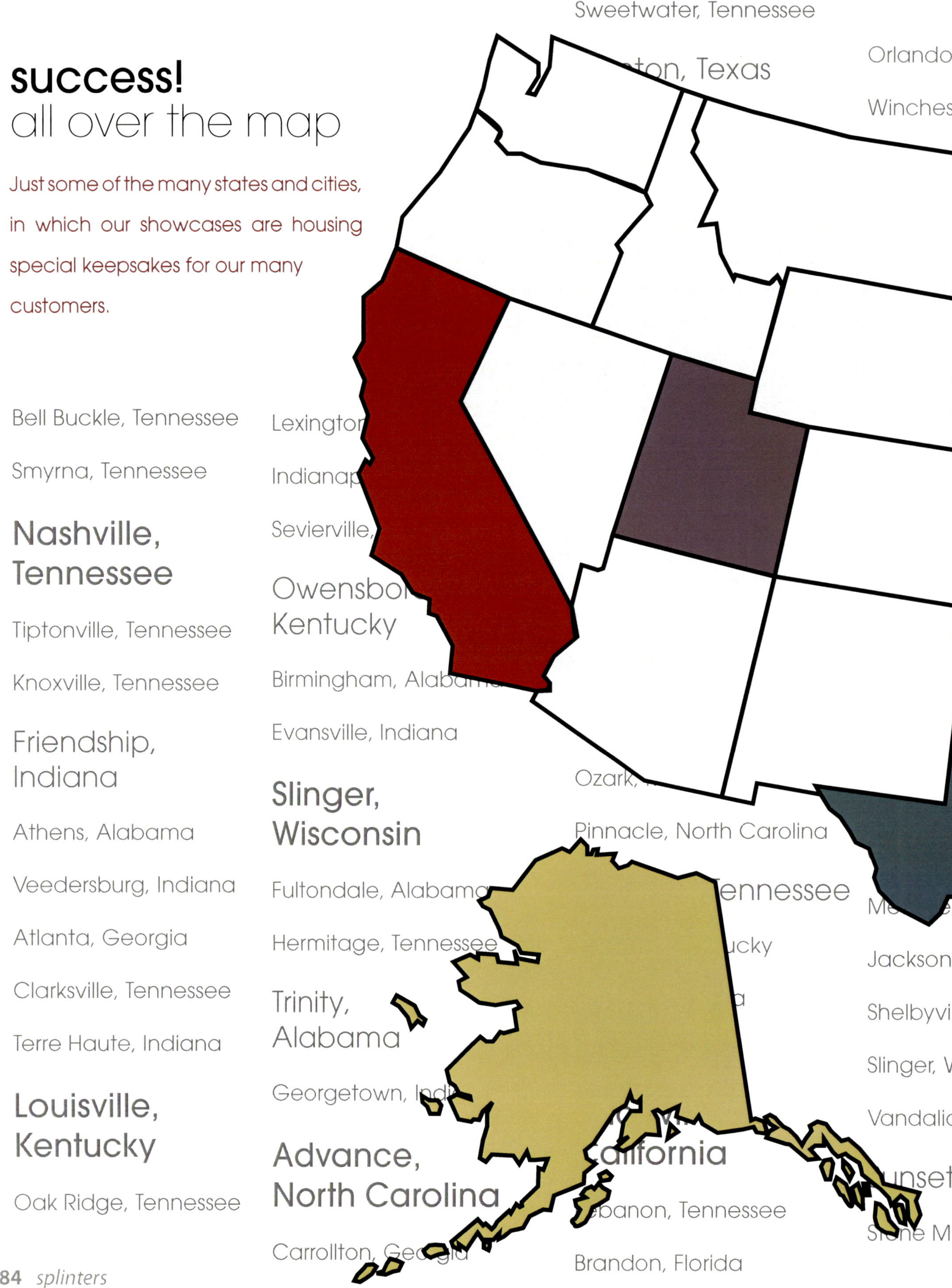

Bell Buckle, Tennessee

Smyrna, Tennessee

Nashville, Tennessee

Tiptonville, Tennessee

Knoxville, Tennessee

Friendship, Indiana

Athens, Alabama

Veedersburg, Indiana

Atlanta, Georgia

Clarksville, Tennessee

Terre Haute, Indiana

Louisville, Kentucky

Oak Ridge, Tennessee

Slinger, Wisconsin

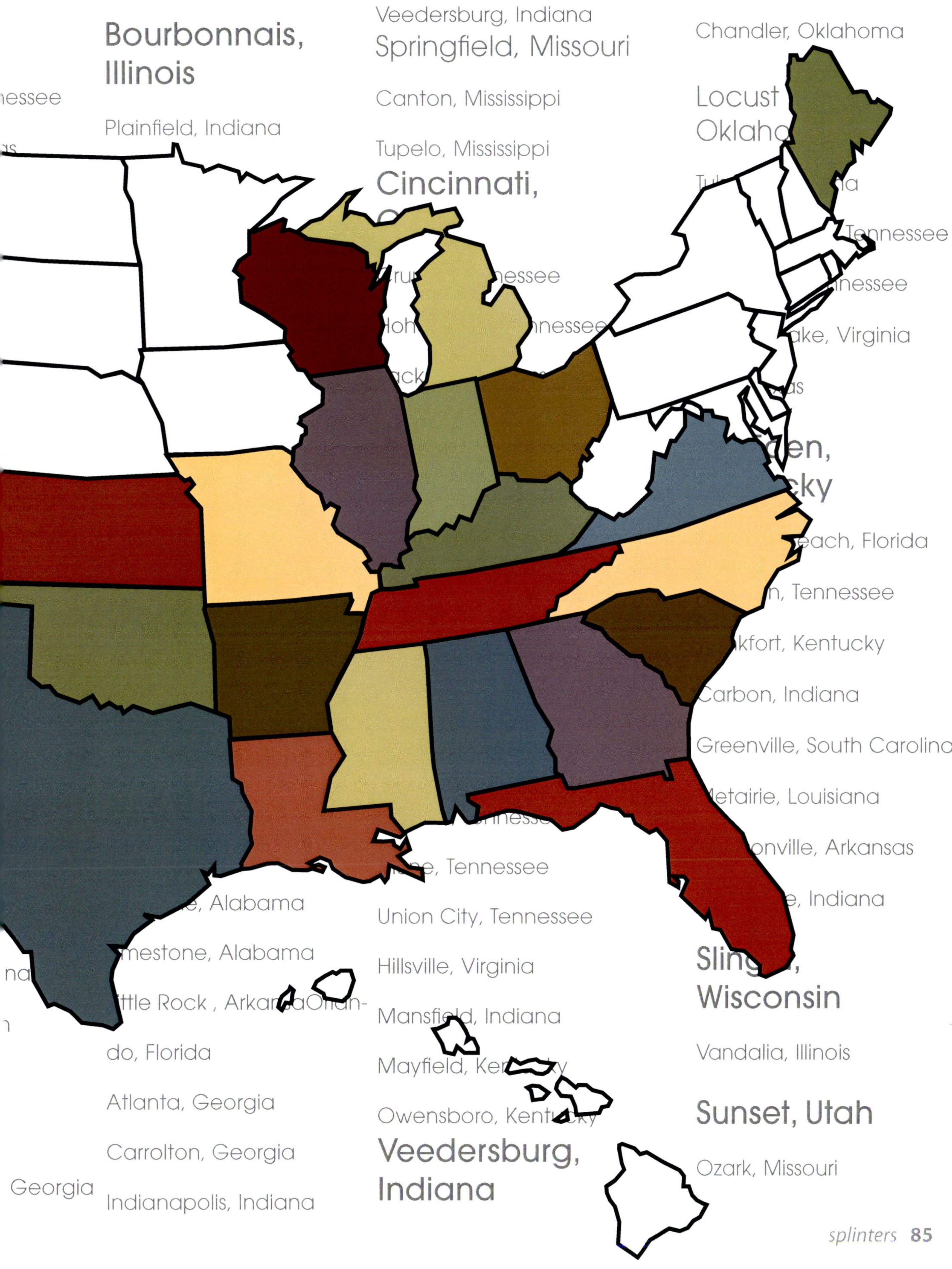

Bourbonnais, Illinois
Plainfield, Indiana
Veedersburg, Indiana
Springfield, Missouri
Canton, Mississippi
Tupelo, Mississippi
Cincinnati,
Chandler, Oklahoma
Locust Oklaho
Tennessee
Tennessee
ake, Virginia
eden, cky
each, Florida
n, Tennessee
kfort, Kentucky
Carbon, Indiana
Greenville, South Carolina
Metairie, Louisiana
onville, Arkansas
e, Indiana
Sling, Wisconsin
Vandalia, Illinois
Sunset, Utah
Ozark, Missouri
e, Tennessee
Union City, Tennessee
Hillsville, Virginia
Mansfield, Indiana
Mayfield, Kentucky
Owensboro, Kentucky
Veedersburg, Indiana
e, Alabama
mestone, Alabama
ttle Rock , Arkansa Orlan-
do, Florida
Atlanta, Georgia
Carrolton, Georgia
Georgia
Indianapolis, Indiana

need for speed

customer profile:
Robert J. Brooks
Nashville, TN

I'm a 59-year-old cowboy, who now lives in Nashville, Tennessee. Prior to 1987 I lived and worked the family ranch in Wyoming. Horsepower has always been part of my way of life. It started with horses, rodeo, and ranching, then came the other horsepower, drag racing cars.

In 1987 our ranch sold and I moved to Florida. Until then I had heard little about NASCAR. Richard Petty and Carl Yarborough were the only names I'd really ever heard. But, being 60 miles from the biggest NASCAR Race, "The Daytona 500," I took up an interest.

The first time I saw Dale Earnhardt Sr. race, I was hooked. Dale was my driver from then on. Dale was The Intimidator, my kind of man, the

greatest driver ever, and is still.

In 1995, I moved to Nashville and Dale Earnhardt collectibles became my big addiction, even though I still owned horses, rode and team roped once in a while.

The pictures show only the cars that Dale Sr. raced, in four different scales. The cars in this collection range in price from the cheapest one I ever found new at $2 to $600. My favorite cars are the blue and yellow Wrangler cars of the 80s 'cause all good cowboys wear Wrangler 13mwz Jeans. But my collection goes way beyond just the cars.

All the cars are kept in dust free oak showcases, supplied by Southern Ladies Showcases. I chose their cases because of their quality material, workmanship, price, and availability. They are the best, hands down, I'll bet my horsepower on them.

candy-filled collection

customer profile:
Ward Tishler
Nashville, TN

When I was two, Santa started to leave PEZ dispensers in my Christmas stocking. My entire family now helps me find all sorts of PEZs! I love going to "Sparky's," which is a PEZ store at Universal Studio's City Walk in Los Angeles, CA.

I have a ceramic doctor PEZ. He has a stethoscope and a light. He is so cool. He even has a small pack of ceramic PEZ candies inside.

My favorite PEZ are my crystal head policeman and fireman. This came out after September 11. I also have the rescue workers collection which is all sorts of people who help others.

My most interesting collection to me is my Star Wars PEZs. I have Han Solo, Luke Skywalker, Princess Leia, Yoda, Chewy, Boba Fett, a storm trooper, Darth Vader, C3PO, and R2D2.

My collection consists of about five hundred pieces. Some of the items I collect are: Chevron and Texaco trucks and planes, Craftsman truck banks, Trustworthy, Shell trucks, WR Case & Son Ertl trucks with Case knives and V&S Hardware banks.

I also have Tennessee Volunteers banks and Smokey dogs and cars; Tennessee Titans trucks and planes and some Coca-Cola banks. I have some Legend Hot Wheels sets and Nascar cars and Gorgie trucks.

fan
pride

customer profile:
Bill Smith
Red Boiling Springs, TN

golden arches

customer profile:
Henry Vaughn
Huntsville, AL

I display my collection of McDonald Happy Meal toys in the cases I have purchased from (Southern Ladies Showcases). I have been collecting Happy Meal Toys for about 15 years but didn't start displaying them until I met Mrs. Howell and began buying cases.

Currently, I have 50 cases filled with the toys displayed on the walls of three rooms in the upstairs of my home.

The toys date back to the mid-eighties through the most recent ones, including the McDonald's 25th Anniversary Happy Meal—THE DOG.

Since I retired from Redstone Arsenal in 1988 collecting Happy Meal toys has become an interesting hobby of mine. If possible

I try to collect one toy of each set. If I miss collecting some of the toys from McDonald's during their promotions I check yard sales, thrift stores, and flea-markets in an effort to collect a complete set.

In December 1997, I was diagnosed with cancer (lymphoma). Since that time I have had many radiation and chemo treatments. In mid-2001 the doctors said I was a good candidate for a stem cell transplant. This transplant was not a complete cure for my cancer but it has given me additional years of life. God has been so wonderful to me and I am very thankful I can still be out and around.

collector, fan, & driver

customer profile:
Dick Boensch
Nashville, TN

(This profile is written from Barbara's point of view)

Since he was a young boy, Dick Boensch has loved cars. He still has the first toy car that was given to him when he was six years old.

"I'm a nut when it comes to cars: big ones, small ones, real ones, toys; it doesn't matter, I just love cars," Boensch said.

Boensch bought his first stock car in 1994 and drove it himself in races throughout 1995. The first race he drove, he won. Heady with this success, Boensch continued to race.

He raced against newcomers Casey Atwood and Bobby Hamilton Jr. during their first races. (Both racers were 14 at the time).

"They had the best that money could buy," Boensch laughed. "All I could do was stay out of their way."

In one of the display cases pictured, there is a car that sits proudly in the case upside down. This is no mistake. That car belonged to Casey Atwood. "In Casey's first Daytona Bush Race, he slid on his top for about one quarter mile down the front stretch," Boensch said.

Casey Atwood's car on the right is proudly upside down.

In 1997 Boensch decided to hire a driver to race for him. Bobby Owens Jr, raced Boensch's 1953 pickup and won the Sport Truck Championship at Highland Rim Speedway in Whitehouse, Tenneessee.

Boensch explained that there are five colored flags in racing. The checkered flag signals a win. The white flag signals one lap remaining. The yellow flag signals caution. The striped flag tells you to move over, and finally, the black flag signals that you are being thrown out of the race.

Boensch has had the pleasure, or dismay, of all five flags having been waved at him at one time or another.

Boensch decided to hang up his keys in 2001 and drove his last race, despite his belief that when you're out there behind the wheel, you have the best seat in the house.

Today, he has happily settled on the sidelines to watch the races and has swapped racing for collecting.

Getting serious about his collection in the 1980s, Boensch has assembled an entourage that includes every model of Chevrolet from 1950s until today, as well as every Corvette.

"At 65, I'm still a little boy with toys," Boensch said. "See the large picture of the 1956 corvette...IT'S MINE!"

On the NASCAR side of things, Boensch's collection includes every major NASCAR driver that has ever lapped a track. In 2009, a museum opening in Nashville, Tennessee will be housing Boensch's collection of model cars and NASCARs all snugly secured in display cases from Southern Ladies Showcases.

"I purchase these cases for several reasons," Boensch said. "The workmanship is super. The display cases makes my cars look good when arranged. And last but not least, they are absolutely reasonable in price."

rocks spark family interest

customer profile:
Jimmy McKennon
Mount Pleasant, TN

I began looking for arrowheads around 1970. My late brother, Bobby Gene McKennon, and I went to Swan Creek on the first hunt of many. We only found a few arrowheads but I found a new hobby. Over the years it became a family affair.

My granddaughter says that one of her earliest memories is sitting in a freshly plowed field with a pail and shovel, while the "big kids" scrambled around to find the first or the best arrowhead, either of which would earn them the bragging rights until the next hunt. This tradition has made it through three generations and we're

starting   on   our
fourth   with   my   great
grandson.

    We hunt mostly close to home.
 The arrowheads in these pictures were found for the most
part in Maury County, usually close to a creek, and the top of Rock
Dale Hill.

    "In the past three years I've discovered 'knapping.' This is taking an
'imperfect' arrowhead and using a tool to resharpen or reshape it. The only
knapped arrowheads in these pictures are the small arrowheads in the box
shaped like an octagon. These I reshaped or added a tip to.

cars of memories

customer profile:
Charlie Dick
Brentwood, TN

(see more on
Charlie on pg 144)

Why do I have my collection? As to the 'why' it probably started with a gift of a 'collector model car' that grew over the years to include a number of cars that have meant something to me during my life.

Most are cars that I have owned or at least driven in—excluding the rare Tucker.

I like to have them displayed for myself but also for the enjoyment of guests to my home in addition to keeping them for my grandchildren and great-grandchildren so they will someday know what 'real' cars were.

I killed this fox squirrel with a 16 Gauge Double Barrel Shotgun in the Fall of 2004 on land in Rutherford Country known as Pilot Knob. This is located in the community of Kittrell, about 10 miles East of Murfreesboro, Tennessee. It was mounted by Gordon Moles of Moles Taxidermy, located in LaVergne, Tennessee.

The fox squirrel is displayed in a walnut hardwood and glass case measuring 12-inches wide; 15-inches tall, and 17-inches in depth. The top lifts off for easy access and cleaning. The case was made by Southern Ladies Showcases of Lawrenceburg, Tennessee.

hunter's treasure

customer profile:
Michael Pethke
Milton, TN

bartering for cases

customer profile:
James Akins
Clarksville, TN

I bought my first model car in 1991. It was a 1930 Packard boat tail speedster, black and gray, 1/43 scale die cast metal. I like the early 1900 models. After the first one I began buying one or two at a time.

In two years I had about two or three hundred cars and trucks. Then I needed display cabinets.

I soon began buying more cars at a time. One day at the flea market I saw oak cabinets that I liked. I made a deal with Barbara Howell. I had a lot of walnut logs.

I traded with Barbara: black walnut logs for show-

cases. I now have 19 showcases that hold 454 cars and trucks. I just ordered two more from Jennifer. I have about 3,000 cars and trucks total. They are scaled from 1/64 to 1/18. I like them all. My favorite is a 1938 Delahaye red convertible.

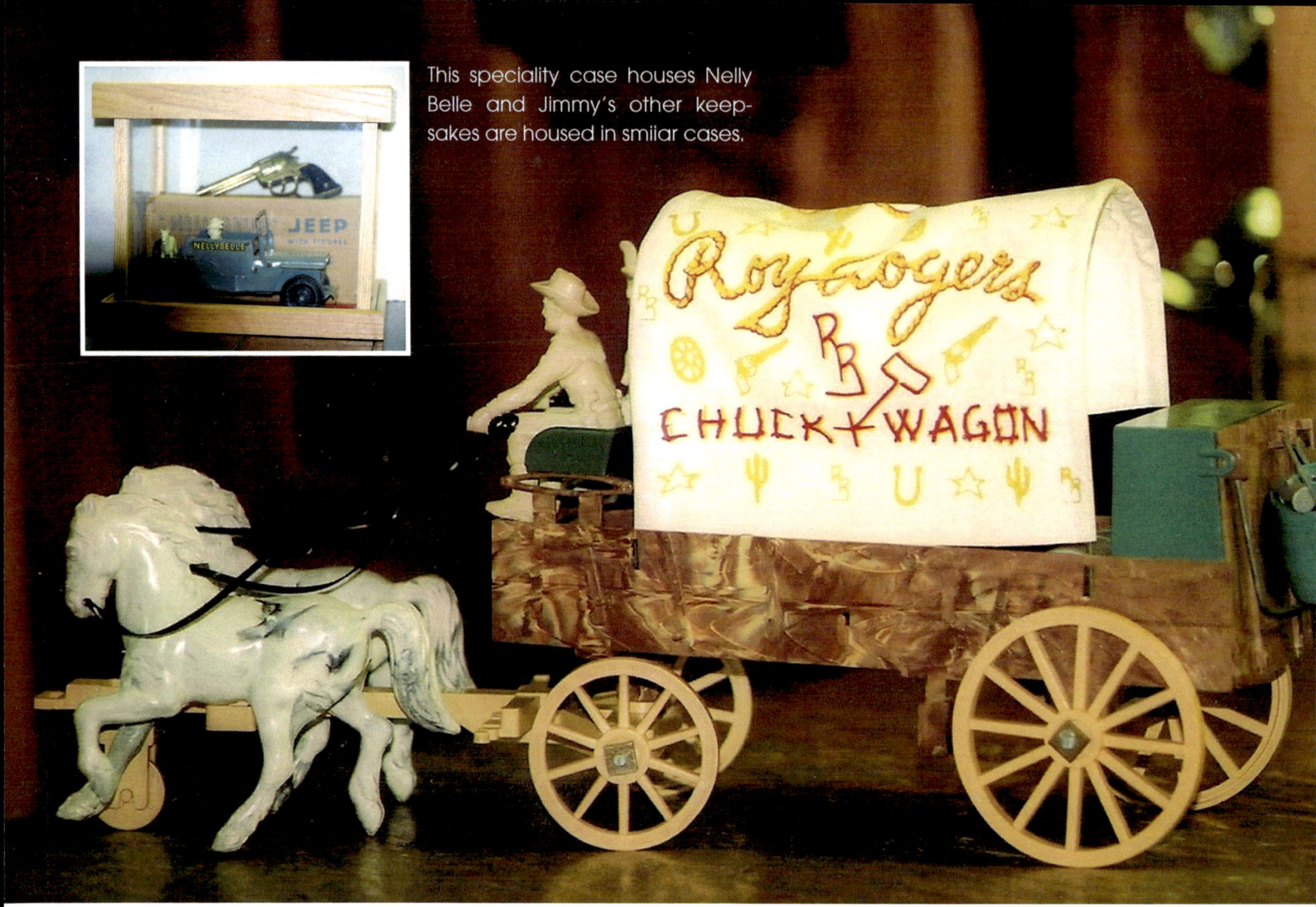

This speciality case houses Nelly Belle and Jimmy's other keepsakes are housed in smiiar cases.

western heritage preserved

customer profile:
Jimmy Judkins
Nashville, TN

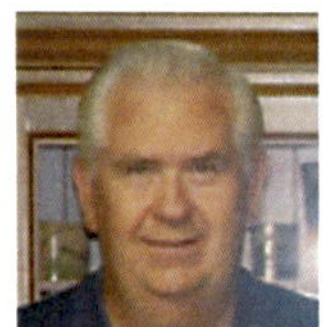

I live in a rural community in middle Tennessee, some 50 miles east of Nashville. I've been collecting for over 20 years.

My collections include stamps, coins, postcards, trains, figurines, plates, and western collectibles with Roy Rogers being primary.

My wife and I have traveled to California to the home of Roy and Dale. We visited the grave site of Roy once and were privileged to meet Dale just before her death.

We go to the western film festivals where we meet fellow collectors. We have also been to Roy's childhood home in Ohio when we went to a festival up there.

There are several items that I am very proud to own. These include original guitars, cameras, a Nelly Belle replica with Pat, Dale and Bullet; Roy on Trigger and Dale with Buttermilk.

These are just a few of the items in my collections. I also have videos and books of the Rogers'.

We have three grandsons and we take them to see the museum and collect western movies for them.

I would estimate the entire collection is worth between $30,000 to $40,000. You can see I'm a serious collector.

Cottonmouth Lures

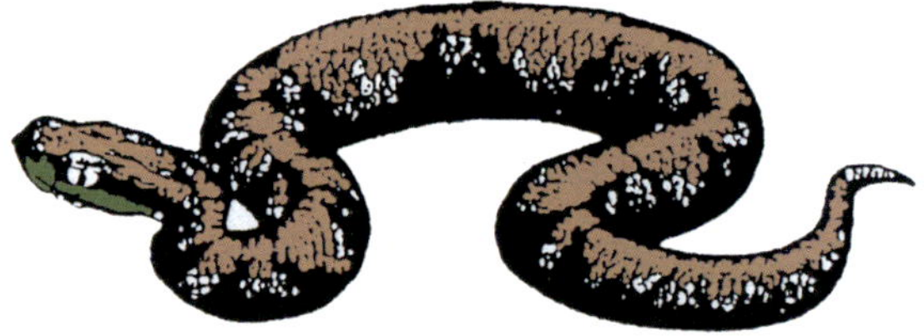

"Building the finest fishing lures, collecting the rest."

hooked on fishing

customer profile:
Fred Washburn
Carterville, IL

I have accumulated about 9700 different fishing lures. I store and display them in large cases from Charlie's Showcases/Southern Ladies Showcases. After buying them we stain them and put foam board covered with burlap or felt in the back. The burlap is stretched and stapled to the foam and the assembly is glued to the bottom of the case. This allows me to pin the lures securely and I can stand them vertically without worrying about tangle or damage.

I have taken the collection to various shows and other places where people who like antiques frequent.

Done right, they make a very impressive display and always draw a crowd. In addition it gives me a lot of relaxation and helps me get away for a while. My collection presently is housed in 164 cases.

cars & trains & collectors

customer profile:
Lewis Frazer
Nashville, TN

(This profile is written from Barbara's point of view)

Though he's only been collecting model cars for about six years, Lewis Frazer's life has revolved around drag racing.

At age 16, Frazer went to work with a pit crew. They would haul and maintain the car all over the nation. Frazer had the opportunity to work all the NHRA drag meets. A few years ago he hung up his pit crew career for Livingstone Racing & Enterprises and started collecting cars instead of working on them!

One of his special collections are a special set of Hot-Wheels that were released by the company. The original plan was to include 96 cars. Hot Wheels ended the set at 80 cars, never producing the remaining 16 cars.

Lewis talks about his cases and collection in this letter he sent:

These are just a few of the 20 or so showcases Mrs. Howell and her granddaughter Jerrica (JJ) have made for me.

The workmanship, or I should say, the work-woman-ship is beautiful. I get them unfinished so I can apply the finish I want. Being retired, I have time to piddle and get things done like I want them.

Having these glass front cases means I don't have to dust all these little cars like I used to, and they're a beautiful addition to any room as well.

So to Barbara and Jerrica, thank you!

HOT WHEELS
Collect Buy & Trade
HOT WHEELS
GL WILCHER
McMINNVILLE TN.
PHONE: 931-473-4121

I first bought cases at the Nashville Fairgrounds. I've got a whole room full of boxes of Hot Wheels, even stacked on the beds.

I've been collecting probably eight to ten years. I started with loose cars at yard sales and flea markets. Now, I've got over 5000 loose ones that you can play with.

I buy the thick cases that don't have shelves because I put the pegs in them and keep the cars in the packages. It will hold 16 that way. They produce 12 Treasure Hunt Edition Hot Wheels a year so I put them in.

I'm partial to the old Hot Wheels from the 80s. I've bought several hundred at a time before when I find a good deal.

full house

customer profile:
George Wilcher
McMinnville, TN

hot wheels
heaven

customer profile:
David Baker
Nashville, TN

(This profile is written from
Barbara's point of view)

David Baker is a unique individual, who has some unique cases and unique cars, as well as several of the match box cases we craft that hold 63 little match-box cars.

As you will note, the insert that houses the hot wheels sign is in stationary position in the center of the case. The cars are placed on each side, underneath and atop of the insert. The dimensions had to be totally accurate, no margin, whatsoever, for error. In most cases, this is totally impossible to design, unless you are an engineer and a woodcrafter combined, which is highly unlikely. You may be wondering how did this case turn out so perfect? There were several factors involved. One: David did a great job in his measuring and designing, and two: there were only four extra pieces involved. Note the beautiful cars.

Dean Bracey buys his cases at the Nashville, Tennessee Fair Grounds. Dean is an avid collector of novelty cigarette lighters ranging from sports themes to holiday collections.

Barbara's business also sells many display cases for Zippo lighters. The Zippo lighters fit perfectly into a 54-slot case that doubles to hold shot glasses.

For novelty lighters though, a much different case is needed. Dean buys cases that have larger shelves so that the lighters can be grouped as desired.

(This profile is written from Barbara's point of view)

mugs & nascar

customer profile:
William T. Byrd
Nashville, TN

(This profile is written from Barbara's point of view)

Mr. Byrd has a great assortment of printed coffee mugs and 1/24 scale NASCAR race cars. He has bought several of the oak display cases from our booth at the Nashville, Tennessee Flea Market.

David is a retired policeman from Paducah, Kentucky. David wanted a showcase big enough to hold all his awards and gun, We designed this case for David, and as you can see, he has it displayed great!

keeping the
peace

customer profile:
David Petterson
Louisville, KY

(This profile is written from Barbara's point of view)

Jen working out of the 24-foot trailer at one of the many "behind-the-scenes" tasks, stapling on backs.

Barbara's personal life has been a roller coaster of ups and downs. Her life as a successful business woman has been the same.

Barbara's many tales of life on the road will bring laughter as she shares stories of duct tape and clothes hangers. They will bring tears as she tells the story of how her dog saved the lives of her and her girls, who became vulnerable during an innocent picnic on a highway.

These stories are true and some are truly unbelievable, like the naked man that sought shelter in Barbara's booth, or the friend, she affectionately calls "The Panty Man," who hit her brand new trailer. Barbara will never forget the day she went undercover with the FBI to unwittingly assist in a sting operation that was housed in her booth.

Throughout the years, she has seen first hand God's protection as she has walked away from serious accidents and mechanical failures that should have left her devastated. She merely picked up the pieces and towed her way to the next show, unwilling to allow circumstances to defeat her.

Take a peek behind the scenes to see the grit, determination, and attitude that has made Barbara a success.

Jen stacking and striping lumber from the Amish to air dry.

Bear stretches from his perch high on top of the radial arm saw to greet JJ when she comes over to measure a piece of wood.

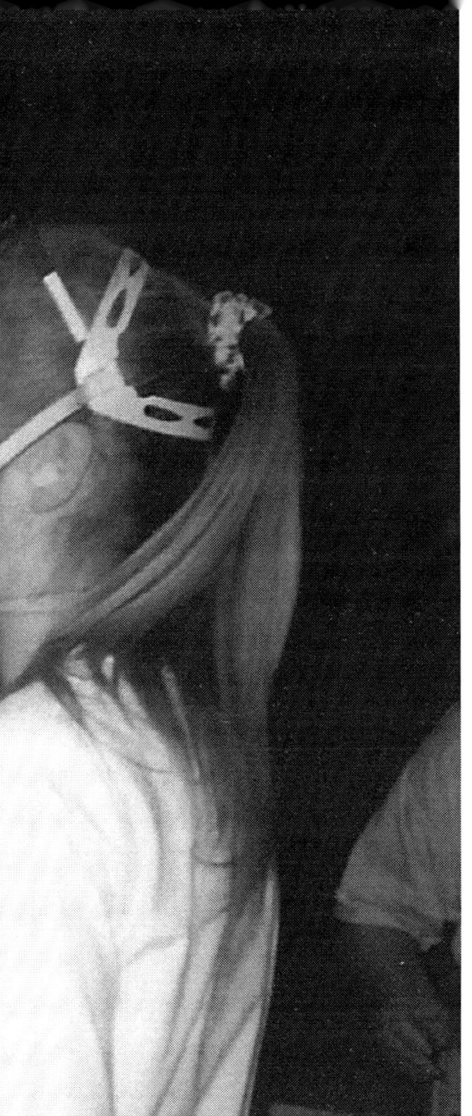

shop cat

The thunder roared. The lightening flashed. The terrorized cry of the small bundle of fur clutching the tree limbs tossed by the wind caught the attention of the Jones girls. Risking the storm's fury, they hurriedly rescued the frightened kitten.

When all dried and safely cuddled, he purred his thanks. Sleek and black as a moonless night, they named him Bear. Bear is a rarity. His first night of terror was nothing but a ruse, for this cat is not afraid of anything.

He sits in their workshop very content. The radial-arm saw is his perch. Occasionally, he'll stretch out his paw for a pat on the head. Bear is a beautiful cat living outside his normal instincts, for he is totally unafraid of noise.

However, he is no misfit, not in this home. Never. For he blends right in with these Southern Ladies who lives outside their normal habitat. For instead of embroidering and sewing, these women operate power saws, six-foot drills and heavy belt sanders, turning out thousands of showcases yearly to house people's valuable keepsakes.

Bear sitting contentedly in his favorite spot watching his girls, Barbara and JJ, run slices through the table saw.

A homeless man's closet.

naked men, duct tape, & clothes hangers

The year was 2002. The location was Sand Springs, Oklahoma.

It was mid-summer and miserably hot in Oklahoma. Barbara and the girls had been camped out in their RV on Key Stone Lake in Sand Springs, Oklahoma, for two weeks now.

The heat wave totally wiped out the battery on her GMC truck. Barbara and Jen had sweated gallons playing mechanic at their first try of putting in a new battery.

Her third Monday morning away from home, Barbara quickly swallowed her last bite of breakfast and closed the door behind her to the fifth wheel. She wiped sweat continually as she made her way to her rig.

She had every intention of sniffing Southern air before this day had ended. True, it had been a very prosperous trip, financial and otherwise.

They had left little unseen in the large city of Tulsa, where they planned to set up residence in the near future. Jen was super excited at getting to tour the campus of the big university where she was slated to begin classes in the fall.

But in all truthfulness, Barbara had to admit this was the hardest trip she had ever attempted.

For one, they rarely did outside shows. Breaking the norm, they found Oklahoma weather to be murder. Gusty winds. Horrible heat. Then a sudden shift in the weather to a shivering cold. All this, happening in one day's time.

Despite all this, Barbara would have to say the bad weather still took a back seat in comparison to her flea market experience in this town.

She had booked a flea market in Tulsa, located several miles from where she was camping. The long drive, back and forth, across the Arkansas river was small potatoes compared to the location of the flea market. Unknown to Barbara, the flea market was located in a seedy part of town.

Barbara was speechless when she learned that a naked man had intentionally taken up residence in her booth one night. Thankfully, Barbara wasn't there at the time!

It happened like this: Barbara closed up early their first Saturday and went back to the campground. Upon her arrival at the flea market the next morning, she was told that the police had been called the night before to haul a naked man out of her booth.

They later found out he was a homeless man and was looking for a place to sleep. She had left nothing in her booth but a straight chair, and after a few hours this proved to get too uncomfortable for the poor old homeless fellow. Thereby, he hatched a plan to get himself a jail bed for the night. He stripped off naked, hoping to get arrested.

He did. Someone saw him and called the police.

What if they hadn't?

Barbara couldn't erase this horrible picture from her mind.

Tulsa, Oklahoma: two weeks in this town had been a plate full, and Barbara was super excited to be going home this early morning. And believing all was well, she turned the key, and put her truck in reverse. She let off the brake and started backing out only to suddenly slam to a weaving stop.

"What on earth was that noise, Jen?" She looked over to her granddaughter who was riding shotgun.

"I don't know, Granny, but it sounds as if the bottom fell out of our truck." Jen quickly jumped out to investigate. "It's the muffler, Granny. What are we going to do?"

"Call Pawpaw, and see if he has any ideas." Barbara knew her husband was a jack of all trades.

Her mind elsewhere, she paid little attention to Jen's conversation with Pawpaw. She was in a tizzy, ready to hit the road with or without a muffler.

"Are you sure?" she heard Jen say, as her mind drifted back to her surroundings.

"Pawpaw said we can wire it up with a clothes hanger." Jen's eyes were sparkling for she was always ready for a challenge.

"Are you serious?"

"As a heart attack, as Uncle Jeff would say," Jen grinned.

"Well, go for it, girl!" Barbara was half-way teasing, for she honestly thought it was an outrageous idea. But before she could change her position, Jen had already made a break for the fifth wheel to get a clothes hanger. Therefore, she decided to keep her mouth shut and hoped it would work, totally aware that most of her husband's hair-brained ideas didn't.

In just a matter of minutes, they had the muffler secured back in place with their made-to-do-tool. The big question was would it endure the 11-hour journey to Tennessee? It did.

No doubt, Barbara has learned how to be resourceful on the road. Even down to the point of helping her friend, Jim, smash to smithereens her own lock to get in her trailer.

Barbara, herding a 58-foot rig became snarled in traffic in just a matter of minutes upon her arrival at the Flea Market in Nashville, Tennessee that busy October day. Security rushed over and informed her she had 15 minutes to unload. And when Jen, who was traveling with her, asked for the trailer key, Barbara realized JJ, whom she had left in Mansfield, Indiana, had the key. JJ and her mom had been left in Indiana to finish out a ten-day show there.

Barbara's philosophy in life is you do what you have to do! And this break-in was small potatoes in comparison to the next issue that came down the pike. This challenge almost took her out. Here she was miles from home, and her trailer was literary coming apart. Unknowingly, Barbara had scattered rivets for miles along a bumpy Arkansas highway. Exposed, the wind had assaulted the naked edges of her tin covered trailer, ripping it down to the second layer of wood.

Barbara was sick upon her arrival in Oklahoma. What was she to do? At first, she didn't have a clue. Later, she got the bright idea of getting larger rivets to fill the stripped holes. But she soon realized there were just too many holes.

Backed by her crew, Barbara refused to give into defeat. And soon these southern ladies had their trailer put back together with beautiful white duct tape. They lit out for Tennessee, hoping and praying their beautiful duct tape would hold for the 11-hour journey.

It did, and not only that, it was holding firm six months later.

Their booth was bustling with activity that early October Saturday morning in Nashville, Tennessee. One particular customer suddenly caught Barbara's attention. She grinned to herself while watching him examine her display cases so thoroughly. Finally her curiosity got the best of her and she eased over to his side and asked, "Sir, can I help you?"

"Yes ma'am. Do ya'll do custom work?"

"We sure do. All we need is your dimensions, and we will get right on it and have it ready for you to pick up next month." Barbara reached out and rescued her order book from the table.

"Great. I'm an archaeologist. I have a large collection of artifacts that I have dug up over the years. I'm most proud of an Indian spear that I discovered, along with some hundred year- old skulls."

"Did you say skulls, like human skulls?" Goosebumps played Barbara's spine as she saw his nod. "Well, like I said, all we need is your measurements."

"Do you have a tape measure?" He asked in all seriousness.

Puzzled, Barbara pulled one from her pocket and placed it in his extended hand.

"Hey, honey," he tap the woman beside him on the shoulder and said, "stand still. So I can measure your head."

Barbara stood speechless as he quickly wrote his figures down. He turned to her and said briskly, "Make me three cases according to these measurements, and I'll pick them up next month." He pressed the tape measure and his figures into her hand and was gone before Barbara could reply.

Above: JJ (left) and Jen pose for a picture with the horse-like dog, Rascal, that helped JJ overcome her fear of dogs.

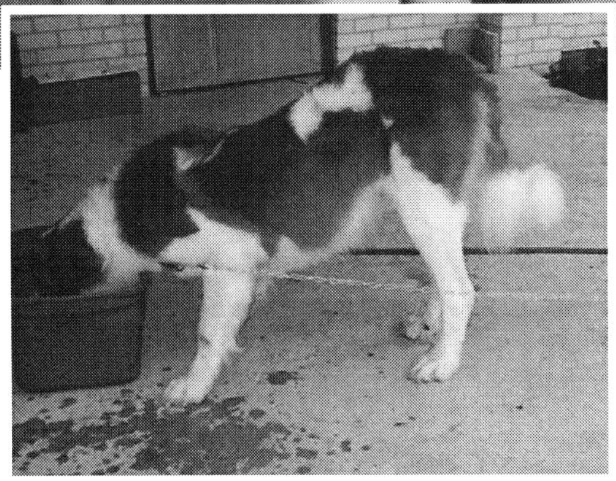

Above: Rascal drinks water out of the only pan big enough for his mighty head, a rubber storage container.

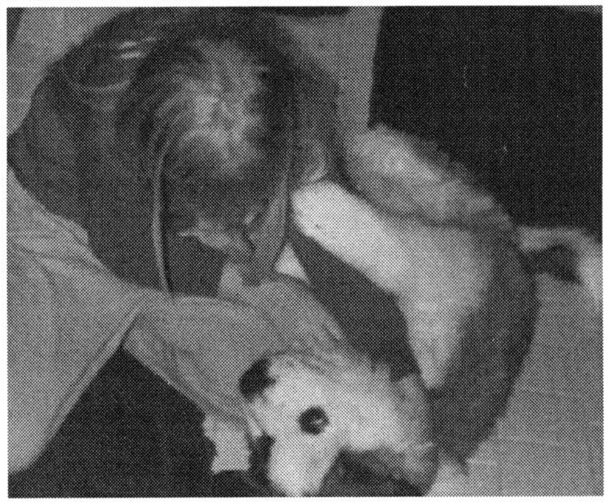

Above: JJ and baby rascal spend some quality time together inside the house. Rascal lived indoors until his sheer size made it necessary for him to have more room to roam outside.

rascal

The two-year-old toddler was busy in her sand box, no doubt building sandcastles. Suddenly, without warning, the child was knocked down, her screams muffled by the sand.

More monkey, than dog, their pet cocker spaniel had climbed his fence and escaped his pen.

Jeannea heard the scream and raced to the scene. She found her child unhurt, but terrorized.

In a few days, the family learned, despite no physical scars, the incident had left its mark. JJ had become afraid of dogs. Big dogs. Little dogs. It didn't matter. If it had fur and a tail, she screamed in panic if one as much as entered her yard. Soon she refused to play outside at all. Her sandbox sat idle. Her swing set was moved only by the gentle breeze that the wind brought. Fear had put this child in prison.

Concerned, Jeannea began to search for answers. She was almost to the point of seeking counseling when someone suggested buying a puppy. Not just any puppy. A large breed. Jeannea loved the idea and put out feelers. Soon a lady at work told Jeannea about a St. Bernard puppy that was for sale in Alabama. This breed was about as big as you could get, Jeannea was told.

The whole family took the trip with JJ to pick out her new friend.

She chose the perky little boy with one black eye. The puppy was a rarity, as most St. Bernard puppies have two black eyes.

JJ cared for her puppy. Soon her fear of dogs was totally erased as she loved and romped with her new friend. She grew to view all dogs as her "Rascal." Rascal was always her baby despite topping the scales at 175 pounds.

Until fully grown, he lived inside the house. Unaware of his height, he often carried the coffee table on his back while chasing a ball. He always traveled with the family. At festivals and trade shows, he received a lot of attention because he was so beautiful and friendly.

The family's greatest pleasure was watching Rascal ride in the Go-Kart with JJ. When he heard it start, he went wild with enthusiasm, sounding his fog-horn-like bark and racing circles inside his pen. Even when fully grown, and much too big for all of him to fit in the double-seated Go Kart, he'd sit upright—the wind blowing in his face, his 16–inch tail dragging the asphalt. He loved every minute of the ride.

Rascal died of heart complications at five years of age, yet he served a divine purpose while here on planet earth. For loving and caring for Rascal not only unchained the young girl from her prison of fear but helped to chart her course for the future. JJ is currently attending her second year of college in Oklahoma, studying pre-med. Her future plans are to become a veterinarian.

The route Barbara was traveling when she had her accident.

the wreck at Bowling Green

Barbara was speeding as she crossed the Tennessee–Kentucky line early that Friday morning. She often wished for eight-day weeks, for she was never ready for a show.

Destination on her mind, Barbara raced right on past the welcoming sign to Bowling Green, Kentucky. However, she did brake when seeing the flashing sign that said reduce speed ahead.

They were traveling caravan as usual. She was leading, piloting a three-quarter-ton GMC pulling a loaded 24-foot cargo trailer.

She glanced her side mirror, seeing her daughter had slowed and had fallen right in line behind her, herding their half-ton Dodge pick-up, pulling a fifth wheel.

Barbara maneuvered to the inside lane eyeing the six-foot concrete wall that now separated the four-lane interstate. She hated the closed in feeling, but quickly realized she was stuck in this lane and was soon forced by the whizzing traffic on her right to hug the wall even closer.

Suddenly, she screamed, "I've lost all power, Jen!" She frantically clutched the steering wheel, seeing her power steering was gone.

"It won't brake!" She pumped the brake pedal to no avail.

"What do you mean, it won't brake?" Jen screamed out in fear.

"I mean, we're moving without truck power. We are being pushed by the trailer. I have to get to the outside lane and off the highway. You watch the on-coming traffic and tell me when it's safe to cross over to the other lane."

Somehow, Barbara managed to get the rig across to the outside lane without an accident. She quickly straightened the rig into a parallel position running with the interstate.

Suddenly, she spied the orange-striped barrels and knew it was just a matter of seconds before she took them out. She didn't one time think to use her electronic brake. She panicked. And in pure reaction, she jerked her gear stick up into park.

Stunned, she realized the truck now made a sudden U-turn and was going back across the highway, heading straight for the six-foot concrete wall. Aware of the terrible danger they were in, she pumped her brakes fast and furious.

Just inches from the wall, she glanced out her side window and saw the semi-truck headed straight for her, broad side. She screamed, "Jesus," fully expecting to see Him in a matter of seconds. She braced herself as best she could for the crash. It came! But not broadside. Instead, she ploughed into the six-foot wall with such force she was jerked straight-up like a stiff.

"Jen, are you okay?" she yelled, in panic.

"I-I think so!" she heard her granddaughter's frightened stammer.

"Thank God! Hurry, and get out of here." Barbara flung her purse out of her path to the passenger's door. She was scared within an inch of her life for now her 24-foot trailer and truck had both lanes totally blocked. And worse, though unbeknownst to her, Jeannea had pulled her rig off the interstate so dangerously close, that oncoming traffic got a first impression there wasn't enough room to pass between them without severe consequences.

Barbara and Jen jumped out of the truck. Barbara slammed the truck door, and made a mad dash for the side of the road only to be grabbed by a stranger asking, "Are you okay? Man, I thought I was going to take you out! I didn't know if I could squeeze between you and that fifth wheel parked over there."

"I'm sorry, that's my daughter. Are you driving that semi with those trucks riding piggy back?" Barbara didn't turn to glance at the semi. It was stamped on her memory.

"Yeah! That's me. Did you have a tie rod end to break?" the young guy asked.

"I don't know. All I know is I lost power and couldn't guide it."

"Well, you have a tie rod end broken now, a flat tire, and a ruined wheel, besides that bent fender. But at least you're okay. Right?" When he was satisfied that she was, the stranger hugged her again, saying he had to be on his way.

She thanked him, and waved, as he looked back in his side mirror, while pulling his semi out on the highway.

"Mom, I've called the police and a wrecker," Jeannea said, walking up to where she stood, not wasting time asking silly questions.

Both arrived in record time. The driver of the tow truck quickly informed them that he couldn't tow both the trailer and truck. Barbara nodded, giving him permission to call for another tow truck.

Minutes later Barbara crawled into the Dodge with Jeannea and the girls and without talk they followed close behind the tow trucks.

"Mom, what are we going to do?" Jeannea asked finally, staring at the wrecked truck as it was being unloaded.

'I don't know yet. Let me check with the man and see what he says about my truck." Barbara turned, and walked toward the garage, Jen flanking her side.

"I'm the lady who owns this truck," Barbara said to the man who was standing beside her injured vehicle. "Can you tell me, when you might get it back on its legs. And maybe give me a ball park figure at the cost?" Barbara eyed the man, summing him up quick.

"We can get right on it, Lady. And I would say, you can count on it being somewhere around $1,500." He spoke with confidence, and Barbara didn't miss the wicked gleam in his eye.

She politely thanked him, and said, "Let me talk to my daughter."

When out of his hearing, she fumed, "He must think I fell off of some turnip truck."

Jen frowned, fearing her granny was getting in a lather.

Upon their approach, Jeannea saw storm clouds on her mom's face and braced herself.

"That man must think I was born yesterday," Barbara hissed, leaning up against the fifth wheel and mouthing off to no one in particular.

"Mom, it don't take a mathematician to figure out you have a 24-foot loaded trailer, and a 27-foot fifth wheel, and only *one* half-ton Dodge vehicle, drivable."

"Well, child, my money is in Louisville, Kentucky. And that flea market is going to open at 12 o'clock." Barbara glanced her watch, seeing it was 11 o'clock on the money.

"Mom, it will start without you," Jeannea said with hope of getting her mom's attention back on her immediate problem.

"It won't be over before I'm there, Honey Child," Barbara snapped.

"I sure want to watch you pull this one off," Jeannea snorted in disbelief.

"Well, come on," she said as she turned, taking long strides without looking back to see if she followed.

"Where are we going?" Jeannea trotted to keep up, halfway wishing she had kept her mouth shut.

"I'm going to talk to the hot-shot mechanic. I'm not as helpless as I look, girl," she said, sarcastically.

"Mom, don't make a scene, please," Jeannea begged.

"I ain't gonna make no scene. I'm going to find out where the KOA campground is."

"Why?" Jeannea stopped dead-still in her tracks, thinking her mom had been injured in the wreck and was having a delayed reaction.

"I told you my money is in Louisville. Now, I'm going to dump that fifth wheel at the KOA campground. Then I'm going to hitch my one and only Dodge up to that trailer, and hightail it out of here. And leave Mr. Opportunist with his mouth wide open, hoping he swallows a big fly," she sneered with a half-grin.

"What are you going to do about the GMC?" Jeannea asked, in full attention now.

"I'm going to call Gary and ask him to tow my truck to Allen's garage in Lawrenceburg. Then after our show, we will come back up Monday and pick up the fifth wheel."

Jeannea's mind went into overdrive. Her eyes were shining with respect as she nodded her head in agreement. She trotted to keep up with mama, for she could hardly wait to see Mr. Opportunist's face upon hearing his rabbit had made a get-away.

Barbara did just exactly as she said, and the cost of repair to her truck was a little over $400.

George staring out the window. Note his protective pose.

The puppy paced the chicken-wire pen showing his dislike of the prison. His fawn colored eyes matched his deer-colored coat perfectly. The Jones girls, excited to be in Georgia, watched him pace. Georgia, nor this huge flea Market, held any attraction for the puppy. He was caged and plainly unhappy.

"Granny, you have to come see him!" the girls gushed, breathless from their run.

Barbara turned, secretly amused, guessing her grandchildren had spied the puppy for sale down the aisle from them.

"Please," they pleaded.

"Girls, do we need another dog? Rascal has only been gone a couple of months." She quickly sealed her lips seeing their unhappiness at the mention of Rascal. Reluctantly, she trailed them to the booth.

They watched the puppy pace. "He's a beauty, I'll give you that," Barbara smiled, soon joining their excitement. "How much are they asking for him?" She didn't miss the spark of hope that struck both their faces.

"Two hundred and fifty dollars," both chimed.

"Too much," she turned to leave.

"No, wait! You can get him cheaper. I know you can," quipped Jennifer, unaware the seller was listening.

"You can have him for two hundred." They turned to eye the man, who had spoken.

"Is he a full-blooded boxer with papers?" Barbara asked.

"We don't have the papers, but we can give you information and you can register him," said the lady standing close by, no doubt her fingers crossed.

"How old is he?" Barbara glanced the frisky pup out of the corner of her eye.

"Twelve weeks. He was sold," the lady stumbled in speech but quickly recovered by saying, "but he was brought back because they couldn't pay for him." Her tale raised no suspicions. They would come later.

Barbara looked down at the small boy, who had walked up beside her, waving money in his hand. She turned and saw the discomfort on the seller's face. She was sorely tempted to step aside. Not to favor the seller. But the boy. For something pulled her heart strings when seeing that little boy's excitement equaled her grandchildren's. Stalling, she glanced down at the boy, then quickly shifted her eyes back to the seller. His greedy eyes spoke volumes as they darted from her to the small boy.

Something, or someone, glued her to the spot. She couldn't walk away. And it didn't have a thing to do with her instant dislike of the sellers, or the joy of watching them squirm.

"Two hundred, you said?" She purposely taunted the greedy couple, which was completely out of her character.

"Yeah," the man grunted, eyeing the boy.

Barbara shelled out the money, not entirely fooled by the man's show of honorability by keeping his word. Yet she didn't gloat about her bargain, and rightly so, for this pooch cost her over $1,000 his first six months of life. And that wasn't the worst! The pup ate an $800 hearing aid before he hit one year of age. But on the bright side, he did leave the battery on the shelf in his mad scramble of thievery. Unaware, he saved his life.

As the pup grew they realized they had purchased a small package with a killer instinct, a killer instinct that would cause two men to ditch their plans of harm to her and the girls while picnicking just outside Jackson, Mississippi.

George. That was the name they chose in honor of his birth state. But his first trip to the vet, he was tagged George Jones. The name stuck. And he is laughingly known as George Jones today.

They discovered he was already house-trained and he quickly embraced their nomad life of travel. His first craft show experience was in Canton, Mississippi.

Barbara leashed George Jones to take him for his first stroll through the busy market.

"Where did you get that pit bull?" She turned and stared at the man who was breathing hard having run to catch her.

"What do you mean, pit bull? You are mistaken, sir. This dog is a boxer. I got him in Georgia, a few weeks ago." Barbara's attitude was somewhat testy.

"Lady, that dog isn't a boxer! That little dog is a pit and a mighty pretty one. Come with me, I have a friend who breeds pit bulldogs. Let her see him, and see what she says."

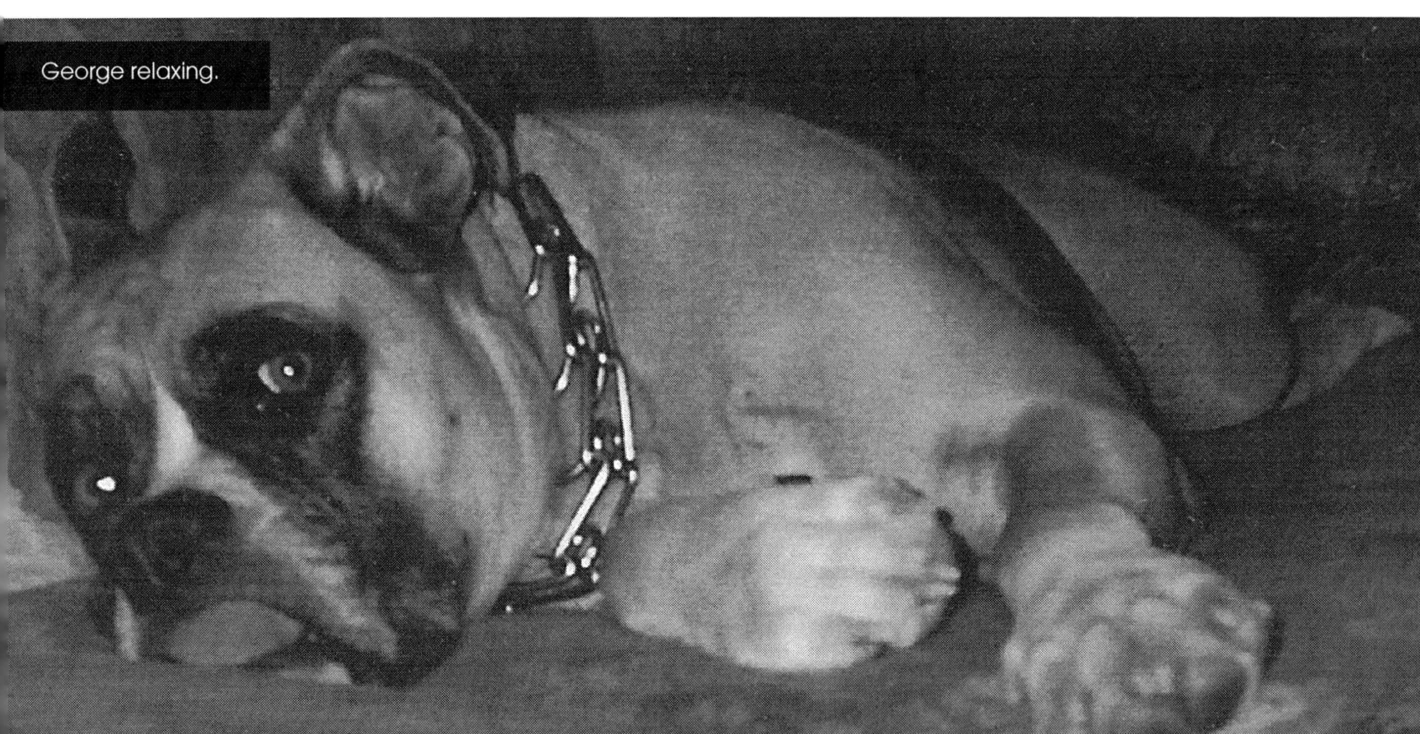
George relaxing.

Barbara followed, fear raking her mind. Something told her the man was right. It fit. No papers. Sold. Brought back. "Sold to children, I'd bet my life," she muttered her thinking out loud. In just the short time they had George Jones, it had been often remarked that they had done the little boy a favor by buying the puppy. Plainly, he was too much dog for a small child.

Barbara lagged behind the man very unhappy. She didn't want a pit bull. Everything she had ever heard about them was bad. Everything. It was factual. They would turn on their owners. She became furious at the couple who had lied to her.

The dog breeder smiled, watching George Jones pull against his leash. "You have a pretty dog," she said, clueless that she was being used to settle a dispute.

"I hear you breed pit bulldogs. Is my dog a pit?" Barbara got right to the point almost rudely.

"Yes." Her answer didn't surprise Barbara or disappoint her new friend, who was now casually leaned up against the tent. "And I would venture to guess one from an aggressive line," said the breeder, adding, "someone has gone to the trouble of bobbing his tail to pass him off as a half-breed. And he might have some boxer in him. But he is more pit. Look at his build. His color. But the shape of his head is the give-away. His dropped jaws could fool the regular Joe into believing he's a boxer. But look at his bobbed tail, which, if you will note, wasn't done properly for a full-blooded boxer."

The lady knew her stuff. Barbara gave her that.

The silence dragged as all eyed George Jones.

"So, I'm a regular Joe, huh?" Barbara said, showing no animosity now, as she grinned at the man propped up against the tent pole.

Later, Barbara trudged back to her booth, the puppy in the lead. She hadn't walked 10-feet away from her new friends before someone hollered, "Lady, is that puppy for sale?" This wouldn't be the last inquiry at the show. Cash in hand, a young boy had tried to buy her doggy at a fantastic price.

George at play.

Barbara wised up fast. She had a prize fighter on her hands, and undoubtedly, she was in dog-fighting country. Had to be! This would only explain all the interest in her puppy.

Granted, her ignorance of dog-breeds had become obvious to her, and plainly, she felt cheated, but her puppy wasn't for sale!

They brought George Jones home and put him in obedience school. He became an official hearing dog for Barbara. He was very protective, and drew the same respect as a sawed-off shotgun. They would become convinced in time that George was their divinely appointed guardian angel. A few years later, without a doubt, George Jones proved this to be true and was elected into their Hall of Fame of memories.

It happened on a trip to Texas their most frightening experience to date.

The show in Canton, Texas didn't start until Wednesday afternoon. It was Tuesday. With time to spare, they were traveling at leisure. They had been on the road almost seven hours. Barbara was driving a three-quarter-ton Silverado pulling a 27-foot fifth wheel. Her daughter was piloting a three-quarter-ton GMC pulling a loaded 24-foot cargo trailer. On a whim, they decided to stop and have a picnic. They were a few miles out of Jackson, Mississippi, when they spied the perfect picnic spot. They pulled their rigs over, eager for food and rest. In glee, the girls made a mad dash for the lone picnic table located down a slope and across a ditch in a shaded area. Laughing and horsing around, the girls yelled for food.

For some unexplainable reason, George Jones was tied on this side of the slope instead of at the table with the girls where he would have ordinarily been tied. Barbara glanced at the dog, thinking how the spikes on his black leather collar glistened meanly in the sun as he waited patiently for his food. He looks so ferocious, she mused to herself as she fixed his food. Again, for some unexplainable reason, Barbara didn't go over to the picnic table. Yet, she had no premonition of fear.

She was chewing her second bite of sandwich, when the red car turned in and crept to a stop. She became alarmed as she watched the two men in conversation. Her fear intensified

George enjoying a Wendy's frosty. He has quite the sweet tooth!

when they made no move to leave. She stood erect in defiance, yet very aware of their vulnerability. Her mind tried to tell her she was being paranoid. Her sixth sense wouldn't buy. She remembered the sign a mile back. The sign, *that plainly* stated, no bathrooms, and pictured one lone picnic table. These intruders could see the picnic table was taken, but they weren't sure who was inside the fifth wheel. This thought raked Barbara's mind.

Time dragged as they showed no sign of leaving.

They had not seen George Jones. A quick glance out of the corner of her eye told her, George Jones had seen them! But strangely he hadn't barked. He just sat on his hunkers very still, his food ignored.

Nervously, Barbara chewed her lower lip as she watched the passenger's side door open. Her eyes never left the scruffy man as he inched his way from the opened car door. When the man was only steps away from his car, George charged—his lips snarled and his bare teeth glistening. His 15-foot lesh almost put him in the man's face.

Barbara heard the man's loud curse and watched him make a mad scramble back into his car. The quick roar of the car engine, said these boys wanted no part of George Jones. As the car sped away, Barbara screamed for the girls to get in the truck and lock the doors. She raced to untie George Jones, who put up resistance, wanting to eat now.

Minutes later when safely locked in their trucks, they all thanked God for his protection and realized they had acted foolishly. However, until this scare, they had been totally unaware of their vulnerability of picnicking on highways. Barbara's mind quickly cast back to the unmolested picnic they had enjoyed last month on a busy Louisiana highway.

Well, there would be no more! She made her declaration known to the group. This was a warning. They would stick to Wal-Mart parking lots.

They hugged George Jones. Of course, he basked in his reward and demanded their kisses.

George Jones traveled every week-end for three years. Long hauls, short hauls, he loved it. His worse trip, was at a NRA Festival in Friendship, IN. The temperature soared to 108 degrees. He was miserable. The show lasted for 10 days, and before it was over, he was eating Popsicles and ice like everyone else. But the sad part, the poor boy came home with the red mange and had to take those horrible treatments.

George Jones doesn't travel much anymore. He is semi-retired. He has a big fenced-in back yard in Oklahoma where he romps and plays with his squirrels and birds, and more or less, thinks he rules the household.

Tennessee state fairgrounds, home of the monthly Nashville flea market.

the panty man

It was the fourth weekend in October

Nashville's biggest flea market show of the year.

Booths are stuffed in every nook and cranny.

Congested traffic usually giving security a fit. In fact, irate vendors have been known to literally come to blows in the parking lot.

Just a few days before this big event, Barbara and Jeannea had made a dash to Bowling Green, Kentucky to pick up their new 24-foot trailer.

In glee, they crammed the shiny white trailer full of showcases. It was money-making time in Tennessee. And this year, they were ready. They were delighted that they had the means to get their showcases to market this year without the hassle of renting a U-Haul.

The October show was their favorite, as well as their customers who were scattered throughout several states. Barbara had made it a practice to ask customers where they lived. And much to her surprise, she found that some lived as far away as, Ohio, Indiana, Michigan, Illinois, and of course, other nearby states to Tennessee were always represented.

The only complaint she ever heard was the traffic jam her customers endured trying to exit I-65. But on the average, most took it in stride and came back year after year.

It was late Sunday afternoon when it happened!

It had been a great show. Barbara and her crew had little to pack. They had moved their new trailer off the parking lot close to their building for load out.

They had paid little attention to the congested traffic as they parked the new trailer. They hurriedly walked back inside and Barbara grinned to herself when she spotted a certain security officer pilfering in their building. She figured right off he was steering clear of the hot spots or so he thought.

Just as she stepped inside her booth, she heard someone yell from the side doorway, "Hey! Whoever owns this new shiny white trailer parked right outside this door, it just got creamed!"

"Oh no!" Barbara screamed out, breaking into a dog run, dodging the last minute buyers, hearing footsteps running behind her. She shot a quick glance back over her shoulder and saw the security officer right on her tail.

She beat him to the trailer.

"It looks fine from this side," she muttered to herself and moved quickly around to the other side. Immediately she spied her friend and from the look on his face, she quickly put two and two together.

"Panty Man! Are you the one who hit my new trailer?" She couldn't hold back her laughter, he was so plainly unhappy and embarrassed.

"I'm so sorry. I just got my new trailer, and I don't know how to maneuver the thing yet," as he was explaining, both their eyes darted first to hers, and then to his.

"Well, it doesn't look like you did a lot of damage to either one," she said.

"I'm so sorry," he bent over to examine the small dent on her trailer.

"Don't you worry one bit about mine, preacher. That little dent is peanuts compared to that knocked-out light, which, I totally demolished on my way up here. I took out one of those orange-striped barrels sitting on the side of the road." Her mockery at herself immediately put him at ease.

The security officer smothered a grin as he eavesdropped their conversation. As yet, he had not said the first word. Instead, he looked from one to the other in amazement, for he had rushed from the building fully expecting to see a free-for-all.

However, he had never seen two people behave any nicer to each other. In fact, someone later overheard him saying just this, and told Barbara.

Barbara hugged her friend and assured him everything was fine. He was really a nice guy and took his nickname well. He sported a laid-back personality and was honestly a preacher. Someone in the flea market had tagged him Panty Man due to the fact that he and his wife sold lingerie.

He and his wife did other shows with Barbara. They were good friends, but to this day, Barbara knows him by no name, other than Panty Man.

Good friends: JC and Betty Franks. Barbara did shows and traveled the market circuit with them for years.

Jim, a fellow vendor and customer. Note Barbara's cases on the table.

A good selection of booths at the Nashville, flea market.

Directing traffic, this gentleman, affectiionately referred to by Barbara as the "Big Man" due to his stature, along with his counterpart, "Little Man," ensures the safety and organization of the vendors at the Nashville Flea Market.

Jackie Freeman's display of her beautiful collection of figurines housed in Southern Ladies' showcases.

covered bridge & jackie freeman

Barbara had heard about the Covered Bridge Festival years before she ever considered giving it a try. To be perfectly frank, she didn't believe the tales that were told about the festival. But all that changed upon meeting one man! This nice, quiet gentleman was set up right behind her at a show close to Nashville, Tennessee, selling socks.

And Barbara saw that he was losing money right and left due to people's impatience and his inability to run his booth by himself. Therefore, Barbara volunteered herself and her granddaughters to help him. Soon, they became friends.

Late that afternoon, after his business had slowed down, he asked Barbara if she had ever been to the Covered Bridge Festival.

"No, I haven't." she said. "Quite frankly, I have never believed all the tales I've heard about it. Is it really true that people can make that kind of money up there?" Barbara eyed him thoughtfully.

"Me and my mama made $30,000 up there last October selling socks." He waited for her reaction with a twinkle in his eye.

He wasn't disappointed, her mouth flew open!

"Are you for real?" She realized she was acting belligerently, and this wasn't her intentions, for she had summed him up early on as being a noble and truthful man. Her opinion hadn't changed despite his outrageous statement.

"It's true. We made $30,000 selling socks last October."

"That was just three months ago," Barbara muttered, counting it off on one hand.

Seeing, she was over her shock somewhat, he said, "One year, it was told, and I don't doubt it one bit, there were a million people come through that show. They bused them in from everywhere. I have even heard that people are bused in from Canada."

"How long does the show last?" she asked.

"You sell for 10 days."

"Okay! I'm convinced! Can you bring me some information tomorrow?" she asked

Jackie has over 100 figurines that she has collected in her travels all over the United States.

with a half grin, and the rest is history.

What a show!

Barbara and her crew walked out with $34,000 that first year.

Covered Bridge Festival is located one hour away from Indianapolis, Indiana, and 30 minutes away from Terre Haute, Indiana, and eight hours away from Barbara's hometown, Lawrenceburg, Tennessee. But when considering traveling time, setting up time, Barbara and her crew are usually gone from home 14 days.

Barbara had to give the show up in 2007 due to not being able to get the inventory while JJ is attending college. She was there seven years and made a lot of friends.

It was at the Covered Bridge Festival that she met Jackie Freeman and her husband. They buy cases from Barbara at the Covered Bridge Festival to house their figurines which have a half marble base and pewter figure on the top. They pick these special gems up in their winter travel. Thus far, they have a total of 100. Their very first one was purchased in Wikiup, Arizona. They stain their showcases and put mirrors on the back. When they are finished the display cases are beautiful.

Residents of Indianapolis, Indiana, the Freeman's fly over the Covered Bridge Festival every year, and Mr. Freeman takes photos for the advertising of the festival, for the owner, Jim York.

Barbara and her crew have always set up with Jim's Parking and Vending, during the Covered Bridge Festival but was unaware of Jackie and her husband's close ties to York.

The relationship goes further back than just the tie at Covered Bridge Festival. Jackie's husband worked with Jim when he was a trucker.

This is such a huge and awesome place, Barbara will always remember their first year at Covered Bridge.

Barbara York, Jim's wife was such a good business woman. She took time and effort to see about her vendors, and she made sure if they needed something, they got it pronto.

Not so with the other side. You see, this show is divided by the covered bridge. You have Jim's Parking and Vending, and then you have the crafts and lots of buildings on the other side, managed by another party. The first year, Barbara set up on both sides. Due to poor management, the other side cost her $100 during the show, simply because they didn't inform her of a certain tax license they were to have in place before the show began.

Later, when unforeseen circumstances occurred in Barbara's business forcing her to cut back on her booth space, she remembered this careless act that never should have happened and chose to move entirely over to Jim's Parking and Vending, due primly to Barbara's York's diligence.

In the past, Barbara has sent countless of vendors to the Covered Bridge Festival. In fact, she gave Jim York's phone number to a fellow vendor just recently in Nashville, Tennessee.

The most touching thing that Barbara remembers is that during the show some years later, Jim's wife, Barbara York, died during a Covered Bridge Festival. However, Jim remained professional and carried on his business, aware he was paid good money in advance by his vendors. (At the Covered Bridge Festival, you pay in advance for the next year if you want to be assured of your spot.)

Barbara's years at the festival are some of her most special memories of life on the road. She will treasure these adventures forever.

Front entrance to the Little Rock Expo Center where Barbara set up for years.

the wreck at little rock

On a Friday night before their show was to start at the convention center the next morning, Barbara, Jeannea and the girls rolled into Little Rock, Arkansas, a little past midnight. They were bone tired and very thankful they didn't have to hunt for a motel. They had reservations at the flea market's guest hotel.

Some of the bigger flea market promoters work with certain motel chains in order to get their vendors good rates and monthly reservations. Fortunately for them, this was one who did.

As Jeannea trudged to the office to get her key and room direction, the girls prayed the room would pass granny's inspection. They were ready to hit the hay, instead of housecleaning. They had stayed in big motels and little motels, cheap ones and expensive ones and had seen the times when neither would pass Granny's inspection.

However, Barbara had grown tired of this hassle, and always came prepared now. She carried her own crisp, clean sheets and blankets, along with a can of comet and gloves. And she hung her little "do not disturb" sign on her door and did her own housecleaning every day she was there. This was before Barbara purchased her fifth wheel.

Inside the room, which looked clean to the sleepy girls, Barbara yanked everything off the bed and went to work, going so far as to turn the mattress to be assured that some druggie hadn't tucked his needle under the mattress the night before. She had one bed changed and inspected to her perfection. She started for the other bed just as the phone rang. She sank down on her freshly made bed to talk to Charlie. Glancing down, she saw an object lying under the edge of the bedspread that covered the bed she was facing. Thinking it was a cigar, she raked it out in plain view with her foot just as Jeannea headed out the door to get another suitcase.

"Forget the other suitcase, and come look at what I've found." Barbara glared down at the soiled tampon.

"I'm going to get my money back, right now! You undress that bed and we will find another hotel," Jeannea was mad as a hatter! She slapped a suitcase in each girl's hand, and was halfway out the door before Barbara had time to move. With disbelief, she was still staring at the soiled tampon.

Of course, as you would guess, they found no vacancy close by. They wound up driving 10 miles out of Little Rock to find a bed. But one thing in their favor, the room was clean as a pin, and Barbara had the mattresses turned and dressed with her crisp, clean sheets in no time flat. Needing toothpicks to prop their sleepy eyes open the next morning, they left early for their drive back to the convention center traveling caravan style. Jeannea was in the lead this time, driving her van. Barbara followed with a half-ton GMC pulling a loaded 10 -foot trailer.

Only a block from the hotel, Jeannea stopped dead-still in the middle of the road. When Barbara realized she wasn't moving, she braked fast but couldn't stop. The loaded trailer pushed her. She quickly braced herself for the crash.

It came. And the noise was loud enough to wake half of the Little Rock citizens from their sound sleep.

Unhurt, Barbara jumped out of the truck and ran to the van. When finding they were all alright, she set into chewing Jeannea for stopping in the middle of the road.

"Well, Mama dear, I yielded and you didn't," Jeannea's voice reeked of sarcasm, now knowing her mom was alright. "I want to know why you didn't?"

"Why would I? I'm traveling a straight road. Besides, I didn't see a yield sign."

"Well, there it is, big as life." Jeannea pointed in the direction of the sign.

"Hun, you're right. But what a stupid place to put a yield sign," Barbara stared in confusion.

"Mom, you have to yield for the traffic coming off the inner state in Little Rock," Jeannea saw her words went right over her mom's head.

"Well, that's the dumbest thing I ever heard. That can get you killed," Barbara raved in disbelief.

Jeannea rolled her eyes and changed the subject, "What are we going to do now?"

"Well, first, we are going to call for a tow truck. And then, I'm calling my insurance to report a very embarrassing accident," Barbara pulled her cell phone from her pocket.

Jeannea grinned big, and asked, "How are you going to break the news to them?"

"I'm going to tell them I kept it in the family." Barbara smirked, and began to punch buttons on her phone.

In just minutes the tow truck was there. When he had them ready to roll, he asked, "Lady, where do you want me to tow this rig? To the nearest GMC place?" By his expression, Barbara knew he expected her answer to be yes. It wasn't.

"No, sir. I want it towed to the convention center."

"The convention center?" Jeannea horned in on the conversation, halfway thinking that her mom might have had a delayed brain injury from the impact of the wreck.

"The show must go on!" Barbara said stubbornly.

"How are you going to get the truck home without it costing you an arm and leg?" Jeannea asked, still not convinced her mom was thinking straight.

"Me and your daddy will come back and pull it home. That way I can have it fixed in Lawrenceburg. The insurance people said it would be okay. Besides, they only pay for one towing any way."

"Well, I guess you're right, the show must go on." Jeannea shrugged her shoulders.

"If you're going to eat," Barbara said, then added, "I'm just glad your van is drivable."

Jeannea nodded and motioned for them to get into her van.

The next week, Barbara and Charlie drove to Little Rock, and towed the truck home. The damage to the van was $6,900. Barbara's truck had a little higher bill. It cost $8,500 to get it back on the road.

But the beautiful thing was, they had all escaped without even a headache.

fort worth, texas

It was late February 2001. Winter was taking a backseat for an early spring in Tennessee. Barbara and her gang were all hustling around getting ready for a big Texas show.

Early one Thursday morning, the weather perfect, they pulled out of their driveway headed for Texas. Their intentions were to break the trip up by spending the night in Jackson, Mississippi. Jeannea was driving a half-ton Dodge pick-up pulling a 27-foot fifth wheel. Barbara was close behind, herding a three-quarter-ton GMC pulling a loaded 24-foot cargo trailer.

The trip went well. They arrived in Jackson, Mississippi, early that evening, and set up camp. The beautiful campground was on a huge lake and budding trees and spring flowers were showing off, encouraged by the mild winter.

The next morning at sunrise, they had the fifth wheel un-hooked from the comforts of home and ready to roll. Forth Worth, Texas, was on their minds. The plans were to get settled in a KOA campground before set-up time at the motorcycle rally.

They hit the city limits in the Texas town thinking they had time to spare. The traffic was heavy but having been there before, that came as no surprise. Barbara kept one eye on the road, and one on Jeannea, because she didn't want to get separated.

Barbara focused on driving and half-way thinking someone had horned in on their channel, she ignored the static groan of her two-way radio. Finally, when unable to endure the irritating noise any longer, she rescued the two-way radio from her shirt pocket and pushed the button for talk

"Yeah?" She released the button.

"Mom, my truck is acting crazy." Jeannea said in a frantic voice.

"What do you mean?" Barbara asked, weaving her trailer, her eyes darting to Jeannea's vehicle.

"The RPM is going wild."

"Dang! It sounds like the transmission might be going." Barbara diagnosed the problem right on the spot, experienced at blowing transmissions.

"What are we going to do?" Jeannea asked.

"We are going to have to find a Dodge place."

"Hey, we are right in front of one! I can see it clear. I don't know exactly how to get to it, but I'll figure it out. Follow me." Jeannea in her excitement, whipped around a car.

Barbara groaned, and followed her daughter, praying they didn't get killed. Soon, they pulled right up in front of a Dodge center all in one piece.

They parked, and Jeannea went in search for help. Soon she came back with some guys, who checked the truck out and said it was definitely the transmission.

"Well, what do we do, Boss?" Jeannea asked, giving her mom the respect that Rowdy Yates would have given his trail boss—Gil Favor.

"Unhook from the fifth wheel, and let them pull it in the shop. But I want a ball park figure of the cost before they touch it." Barbara said, without thinking, for at this point it didn't matter what it cost if they wanted to get back home.

"Is it still under warranty? Jeannea asked, hopeful.

"Probably not!" Barbara smirked.

Later, Jeannea and Jen trotted back to where Barbara and JJ were waiting in front of the fifth wheel.

"Mom, it's still under warranty," Jeannea said, with a smug smile.

"What's so funny?" Barbara eyed her daughter.

"You are not going to believe it. The truck lacks 36 miles being out from under warranty. The guys are all laughing, because Dodge is having to honor it, and the boss man ain't happy."

"I told you we are blessed," Barbara roared in laughter. "Listen, how many Dodge transmissions blow right in front of a Dodge service center? And furthermore, with only 36 miles left on the warranty?"

"Well, we aren't going to make it to the motorcycle rally. It's going to take several hours to do the job. That means, you will lose your $200 set-up fee," Jeannea frowned, hating to be the bearer of bad news.

"Nay. We aren't going to loose our $200, Jerry Savelle's ministry is good soil. If these boys can get us back on the road by late evening, we will take a dash right down I-20 to Canton, Texas. This is First Monday Trade Days weekend. We can catch the last day of the show. We won't lose anything," Barbara said with glee.

That is exactly what they did! They didn't walk away empty handed either. They came home with $1,300 of Texas money and a new transmission. A very memorial Texas Motorcycle Rally, wouldn't you say?

the first meeting
with charlie

Barbara's first meeting with Charlie Dick was rather dramatic. In fact, you could say it was down right humorous.

After she has gotten to know Charlie and love him, she knows that Charlie was just being Charlie that day.

On this particular occasion, Charlie came into their booth, mouth first.

He spied their 1/24 scaled car case.

He pointed and said, "That case won't hold a 1/24 scale car."

"That case will hold a 1/24 scale car," Barbara emphatically contradicted him, experienced at being put down by know-it-all men.

He began to argue and blatantly said, "I'll bet you $5, it won't hold a 1/24 scale car."

"That is a 1/24 scale car case, and I can prove it, and I will take your money, sir." Barbara held her ground, with intentions of taking his $5, as she had from the know-it-all-man in Atlanta. That man had come into her booth in Atlanta, Georgia and bet her that the thimble case would hold golf balls. She tried to tell him that the dimensions were a tad smaller, and it held thimbles. However, he wouldn't listen.

Thinking, this was the same scenario, Barbara turned to Jen and said, "Get one of our 1/24 scale cars and prove to this man this shelf will hold 1/24 scale cars."

Charlie looked first at Jen, and then to Barbara. Finally, he said, "That case will not hold my 1/24 scaled cars."

"Do you own 1/24 scale NASCARs?" Jen asked, as she held up the car.

"No." And he immediately began to describe his collection.

Barbara realized the problem and casually moved out into the aisle to join Charlie's friend letting Jen handle it.

A poster advertising the movie based on Patsy Cline and Charlie's life.

One of Charlie's display cases of cars.

"Do you know who that is that you're talking to?" the man asked, eying Barbara.

"No, sir, I don't. But it doesn't matter, I know my cases and their capability."

"That is Patsy Cline's husband. And I'm Norma Jean's ex-husband," he said, rather proudly, referring to the two female country music stars.

"Well, I thought all ex's lived in Texas," Barbara flippantly brushed him off, borrowing a line from George Strait, never giving it another thought.

Barbara is an avid reader. She reads every night before falling asleep. A few weeks later, snuggled in her queen-size bed in her travel trailer, Barbara picked up the new book she had recently bought. It was Loretta Lynn's autobiography. When she got over to the chapter of Loretta's friendship with Patsy Cline and her husband, Charlie Dick, Barbara stared at Charlie's name, remembering vaguely what Norma Jean's supposedly ex-husband had said.

"Hey, Jen, get our order book from Nashville and bring it to me."

"Why?" Jen asked, as she fished in the filing cabinet for the book.

"I want to look up something!"

"What?" Jen's interest was now sparked, and Barbara told her of her conversation with the country music star's ex-husband.

"Granny, you are pulling my leg, right? You didn't slur that man by saying all my ex's live in Texas, did you?"

Barbara didn't admit to anything verbally but tossed her granddaughter a sly grin.

"You did!" Jen groaned.

Barbara hurriedly raked through the order book. She smacked herself upside the head, saying, "I swear the man was telling the truth! Look! Charlie Dick is the name you have written down on our order book."

"Well, Charlie may not come back and pick up his case if he finds out that you slurred his friend," Jen couldn't resist a dig at Granny.

"Naw, Charlie didn't strike me as being that kind of a fellow," Barbara handed the order book to her granddaughter and went back to her reading.

Well, Charlie came back the next month and picked up his case and ordered another one. They never let on that they knew who he was. This went on for several months.

Sometime later, Charlie placed an order and when he came to pick it up, he started in with, "How much of a discount are you ladies going to give me?"

Barbara grinned, and said, "Charlie, you don't need a discount. You got the money!"

She cut loose singing, "I Go Out Walking After Midnight," one of Patsy's biggest hits, and Barbara's favorite.

He laughed and paid up without another word.

Charlie comes by to see Barbara and JJ, just to jaw when he comes to the flea market. He is always a ray of sunshine and hasn't changed one bit. He still comes in mouth first. But they love his stories and his gusto for life.

Barbara's booth at a typical outside flea market

working undercover with the FBI

The sun had made an appearance early that day. Barbara and the girls were set-up at an outside show in Bessemer, Alabama. Wiping sweat, Barbara figured the day to be a scorcher and a bore.

Barbara wished for her tent as she cast envious glances toward her neighbors two booths down.

They looked so comfortable sitting on their shaded porch amid all the beautiful Nike and other name brand T-shirts. From her vantage point, Barbara could see they were well-stocked with other merchandise, also.

There were several guys minding the store, no doubt savoring the rush of their early bird's sales. Barbara couldn't help but compare her mite and the absence of customers.

To be truthful, she had one lone customer.

One lone customer, who had already picked up every case in her booth and carefully examined each one with a fine-toothed comb.

After awhile, Barbara went over and struck up a conversation with the young man. She talked and talked, and he finally made his choice of a couple of display cases. And then, he strangely and casually asked, if she would mind if he hung around for awhile.

Barbara said no, assuming he was waiting for someone to meet him.

Soon, Jen got suspicious. She mouthed to Barbara, when his back was turned, that her customer was weird.

Barbara nodded with a grin but kept on talking to him about this and that and nothing in particular.

After one hour, he asked, if he could leave his cases and pick them up later.

"Sure," Barbara told him and didn't pay any attention to what direction he went when he left her booth.

In a few minutes, stunned, Barbara and the girls watched as guys ran past their booth in their FBI jackets.

Seconds later, Barbara's eyes ran out on stems as she recognized her long-staying customer coming down beside her booth dressed in his FBI jacket herding a man in handcuffs.

As he passed her, he flashed a big grin and kept on walking without speaking.

When recovered, Barbara said, "Well, Jen, I guess he wasn't so strange after all. I wonder what those dudes have done that the FBI is after them."

"I don't know," Jen said. "But didn't the FBI guy leave his cases here? Maybe he'll come back and tell us."

"That's why he was hanging around our booth. He had that house staked out and was waiting on the rest of the guys. I saw some guys running from the house just minutes before the FBI boys ran past our booth."

"We didn't," both of the girls chimed.

"I didn't think anything about it." Barbara admitted, still watching customers scatter in haste from the tainted booth.

After awhile, their friend came back still wearing his FBI jacket and was grinning from ear to ear.

"Yeah, you're good, Mr. FBI Man. You totally fooled us." Barbara teased him. "Now, that I know what you were doing, you don't have to take those cases."

"No, I really want those cases. How much do I owe you?"

Barbara told him.

And then she said, "I'm curious. What was going on with those guys in that house?"

"Plenty. They are well organized and have underground factories here in the United States. They copy all their stuff, make it cheap, sell it cheap, don't pay taxes, and it hurts the American economy something fierce."

"What is going to happen to them?" Jen asked, feeling somewhat sorry for the bad guys.

"Very little. I might add, we have confiscated all their stuff, which filled two semi-trucks. They will have to make a $1,500 bond. But, they will be out of jail in a few hours. Then, they will just find another location and begin the game all over again. We aren't getting rid of them, but at least, maybe we are hurting their pocket book."

"How long have you guys been watching them?" Barbara asked, realizing he didn't mind their questions.

"We have had them staked out for three months."

"Well, I want to ask you a personal question," Barbara said, grinning. "Since I've helped you, unknowingly, don't you think that entitles me to one question?"

They all laughed, aware how they had done nothing but pump him with questions since he had come back to their booth.

Good naturedly, he eyed her and said, "Shoot."

Barbara related the story of how Jen had helped a guy the week before in Jackson, Tennessee. She told him how they began to get suspicious of his merchandise when on Sunday, he wouldn't uncover after they had told him that they had heard the FBI was coming.

"You haven't asked me a question yet," he prodded.

"Oh. I want to know, what would have happened if Jen had been helping him, and you guys raided him?"

"She would have been arrested. And she would have been taken to jail."

Jennifer turned white as a ghost, but recovered quickly and quipped, "Well, the guy did give me a T-shirt. Can I be arrested for wearing it?"

He laughed and said, "No."

Barbara became serious again, and asked, "Are we okay with our little stools that we have painted Disney characters on?"

"Yes, they are hand-painted on wood, and you don't have any names on them."

"Do you usually find this stuff in smaller markets like this one?"

"Yes." And he went on to explain, "These folks had everything from Rolex watches to all sorts of copyrights."

Soon he made his get-away, thanking Barbara and the girls for the use of their booth, warning them to be careful.

Barbara and the girls could hardly wait for the day to end. They were looking forward to sharing their adventurous day with the rest of the family, who were set up at the fairground in Birmingham, Alabama.

A barrel of welcome to Monday Dog Day.

monday dog days

It was the middle of a hot, sticky Tennessee summer. Jen and Barbara didn't mind, they were doing what they did best—they were making money.

They were at a show that most folks would say was located in the backwoods of Tennessee. It could be said, and in all probability be the truth, that this flea market had once upon a time been a cow pasture but not in several years. Monday Dog Days in Ardmore, Tennessee, is known far and wide.

The owner, Alex James knows his business. He has worked both sides of the street so to speak. Before buying this flea market, he traveled extensively selling antiques and has an antiques barn on his flea market grounds in Ardmore.

Barbara has met some great folks at Monday Dog Days and has accumulated some funny stories.

She has two distributors whom she meets there to re-stock. One drives over 100 miles and the other drives 50 miles. She found this little flea market over four years ago, and when not on the road, she is there almost every Monday.

One of her Alabama vendors is hilarious. She calls him "The Hustler." Quite frankly, she doesn't even know his full name. She met him at Dog Days right after she went there in 2004.

He called her one day and said he wanted to become one of her distributors. He said he was a "hustler" in business. Then he related the story of how he had taken a truck load of barnyard manure to a flea market in a little town just outside of Nashville, Tennessee. He bragged about how he had sold that whole truck load of Alabama barnyard droppings to those Tennesseans.

Barbara got so tickled hearing his story that she signed him on immediately. She quickly realized that he hadn't oversold himself one bit. He was a go-getter.

He has had diabetes ever since he was five years old. There is little doubt in Barbara's mind but what this young man could become a millionaire if his body would only cooperate with his mind and attitude.

On several occasions, he has met her and JJ at the Ardmore Dog Days show and tried to pull one over on JJ, by asking her to price him the whole booth except the tables and tent.

She'd do it! And she'd get a good price with no advice whatsoever from Barbara. The hustler would just laugh, and pay up to the 17-year-old, fully aware she knew her business.

Mr. James happily collecting booth rent money.

The big Antique Barn located at the flea market at Dog Day.

Antiques inside the antique barn.

Part of Barbara's booth at Dog Day.

...ntiques and more antiques, Mr. James is very experienced in the antique world, having traveled extensively all over the United States selling and buying antiques before he became the owner of Monday Dog Day.

Louise Smith and David Elder at the International Motorsports Hall of Fame in Talladega, Alabama in April 2004. Louise was inducted into the Hall of Fame in 1999.

few and far between

Another interesting character that Barbara has met at Dog Days is David Elder.

The people you can trust these days are few and far between. However, Barbara found David not only to be honest but a person of great interest.

David became a racing fan at a very early age. His mother used to take him and his little sister to the old Music City Fairgrounds, located in Nashville, Tennessee. There was a small theme park there, and on the weekends, different types of races were held, such as stock cars and 18-wheelers.

Tim Mitchell & David Elder posed with car #06 beside the race track.

Today, David is the proprietor of Team Elder Motorsports, which is no great surprise considering his early years of exposure to stock cars racing.

In 1991, David started working in a collectible shop and often went on the road doing Racing Collectible Shows.

Stock car racing in his blood, and this experience under his belt, two years later he struck out on his own and formed Team Elder Motorsports, specializing in racing cards, autographs, inserts, parallel promos and samples, hard to find items, and diecast.

David is a member of N.U.T.S. (NASCAR Underground Trading Society), as well as, ARCA (Automobile Racing Club of America). David's whole life is consumed with racing in some fashion.

In 1993, working a collectible show in Greenville, South Carolina, David got the opportunity of a life time. He got to meet personally, the "First Lady of Stock Car Racing", Louise Smith.

She was a down-to-earth kind of lady, and they soon became close friends. He was there and shared her joy when she was inducted into the International Motorsports Hall of Fame in Talladega, Alabama, in April of 1999.

Louise Smith was one of the "new breed" in her time. She had never seen a stock car race before she drove in one. Nobody told her what the checkered flag meant. Finally it dawned on someone, that she didn't know, and they grabbed a red flag and stopped her racing against herself.

In 1946, Bill France arrived in Louise's hometown, promoting a racing circuit that was to become the National Association for Stock Car Auto Racing (NASCAR). France thought getting a woman to drive in a race would be a great publicity stunt for the Greenville track.

The local track manager suggested Louise Smith. He told France, "She is the craziest one we've got around here." Going along with this far-out idea, Louise later become the first lady of stock car racing.

David remembers, in December 1994, that he had hit a bad time in his life. He was in a bad automobile accident. His car was demolished, he was hurt and unable to work for a time. What did this grand lady do for her good friend?

She sent David her die-cast racing cars to sell, while he was recovering from his accident. During the Thanksgiving season of 1997, David visited Louise in her home. An avid storyteller, her many tales of life on the track and beyond often put him in stitches. He kept in close touch with this remarkable woman until she died in 2006.

She was certainly a legend in her own time, racing on dirt tracks from the southern United States to Canada for 11 years. She won 38 races. She started in 13th place in her first race on the beach at Daytona. She had sand kicked in her face from the tires of Lee Petty and Buck Baker. "You couldn't see anything," she said. "The sand was knee deep in the North turn." With this horrible disadvantage, Louise finished as she started— in 13th place.

Louise's grit and determination is the substance of any winner. She was often heard saying, "I won a lot, I crashed a lot, and I have broken just about every bone in my body, but I gave it everything I had."

Barbara and the late Louise Smith share a common bond. Both learned how to make it in a man's profession and still maintain their femininity. David has been in business over 15 years. He has met people from all walks of life. He bought showcases from Barbara for his business and also for his own personal die cast. And one of his favorite shows to visit is Monday Dog Days.

June 10, 2004

Dear Barbara,

Thanks again for your trust in me, that is something that some people have a hard time doing these days due to the way our world is going. I do want to have some cases made, but would like to come there to talk about the layouts. The case I bought is well built, and I really like the sliding glass feature.

Thanks again,

David B. Elder

Daniel Wiley

Jeremy Gallaher

Nick Eledge

Jon Wilburn

Colby Eledge

the best of the best

Southern Ladies Showcases is a family-oriented business.

Early on, Barbara turned a phase of the business completely over to her granddaughters, such as the grading, gluing, and nailing. This was a big and important step of the process in making display cases. The girls got behind in their gluing due to the demands of their school work. Barbara came to the realization that they needed help.

This business was housed inside the privacy of their home. This made the decision to bring in employees much more complicated. Barbara didn't want to hire some "Joe" off the street. So after much consideration, she called the local high school principal. She asked him to announce to the woodworking class she would hire some of the students for work after school. That very afternoon, Daniel Wiley and Jason Clanton came by and applied for a job.

Jason decided after two weeks he didn't care for woodworking. Daniel stayed and made an excellent hand, later recommending his good friend Jeremy Gallaher, who came in for the long haul with fantastic work ethic.

When Christmas rolled around, Barbara told the boys her Christmas present to them was furnishing the material and machinery, and they could make anything they wanted to make, either for themselves or for someone else for Christmas. They each chose their item and made it from start to finish.

They graduated and moved on, leaving lots of good memories. The next school year, Barbara hired Nick Eledge and Jon Wilburn, also from the high school woodworking class. Both had a talent for woodworking. Nick could use a nail gun with the expertise that he could pick a guitar. Jon could figure square footage in wood and run a power saw or power feeder as good as any experienced carpenter.

Barbara pulled a trick on Jon and Nick one afternoon after school. She had a customer who had bought several cases and happened to be the sheriff of an adjoining county.

He had recently ordered a load of display cases and wanted someone to meet him at the jail for pick-up that afternoon. Barbara called and asked him if he would mind giving her young employees and granddaughter a tour of the jail. Of course, he said he would be happy to do this.

When they arrived home from school that afternoon, Barbara had them sign in. She would pay them their regular wage for the time they were gone. Thinking they were just making a delivery, they were not the least bit suspicious. After they got to the jail, a hilarious thing happened. Jon's phone rang. It turned out to be his aunt, and of course, her first question was, "Where are you?"

He got a big kick of telling her he was in jail. Soon, he let her know he was only there as a visitor. The trip was a sobering experience for all as the sheriff laid it on pretty thick. They all got his point! They told Barbara, they didn't ever want to be confined in jail. Ironically, they continued to talk of their trip to the jail for days.

Once these two moved on, Barbara hired Randy Jones. He was an experienced carpenter. This was just a fill-in job for him, while he was between jobs. However, he was a God-send and worked for several months and helped Barbara pull a big show together that would have otherwise gone begging.

At Randy's leaving, Colby Eledge, Nick's brother, came to work for Barbara. Colby was worth a million dollars putting on hinges. Colby had played baseball in high school. He won a college scholarship and played for the school until a severe arm injury ended his career. Colby could no longer play ball, but he still had the muscle power of two men. It was exciting to watch him work. This boy sparkled with life. He loved deer hunting with a passion and was good at it. He worked with Jen after school, but he also worked some during the day, as he was in the middle of a transfer in his college career.

One day, he and Jen came up with the bright idea they would enter a duck stamp art contest. He hurried home during lunch break one day to get all the information for her before she got home from school later that afternoon.

In his rush home, he got a speeding ticket. When he got back to work he told Barbara that he was going to tell Jen she had to pay half of his ticket. Barbara doesn't remember what happened with the ticket, but they entered the contest and though they didn't win, they made some good memories.

Sad to say, after Barbara and her gang relocated to Oklahoma, Colby was killed in a tragic car accident. Barbara and her gang will never forget these young guys and will always cherish their fond memories of them.

Billy Phillips of M.L.Sandy Lumber Co.

hometown heros

Billy Phillips, Barbara's hometown manager of M. L. Sandy Lumber Sales Inc., became her good friend, and often went the second mile to help keep her stocked with certain supplies. M. L. Sandy's and their staff were just another example of the help and encouragement Barbara got behind the scenes.

David Brewer, employee and Billy Phillips manager, M.L. Sandy Lumber Co.

A few years ago, Barbara was on her way home from a long haul in Texas. Her truck's engine light came on signaling a problem. Upon her arrival home, she discovered that she had an oxygen sensor gone bad. Who could fix it? Her local Auto Zone recommended Jobbers Supply. To Barbara's surprise, she found that an old school friend Charlotte and her family owned this business. They had a great time sharing school days, especially hashing their memories of their sophomore year. Barbara and Charlotte were best of friends their whole second year of high school and ate lunch together every day.

Barbara enjoyed the renewing of friendship with her old school pal. Today, Jobbers Supply keeps her truck fine-tuned for the road.

Jobbers Supply
918 N. Military Ave.
Lawrenceburg, TN. 38464
Phone 931-762-7862

Special Thanks!

Barbara Howell became a successful woman in a man's world. But Barbara would be the first to admit that she has had lots of help along the way. For this she sends her many thanks to all.

Tennessee Valley Wood

H.B. Brink & Co.

Augustine Lumber Co.

Hassell and Hughes Hardwoods

M.L. Sandy

Lawrenceburg Glass

Chapman Tires

Jobbers Supply

Allen Engine and Machine

South End BP

Cash Moulding of Birmingham

Her Amish Friends, Daniel & Neil Miller

Robert Hayes & Son